Hello Hello

A Romantic Satire by Karen Hines

Score by Greg Morrison and Karen Hines

Coach House Books, Toronto
2006

First edition

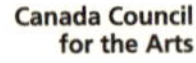

Published with the assistance of the the Canada Council for the Arts and the Ontario Arts Council. We also acknowledge the Government of Ontario through the Ontario Book Publishing Tax Credit Program and the Government of Canada through the Book Publishing Industry Development Program.

LIBRARY AND ARCHIVES CANADA CATALOGUING IN PUBLICATION

Hines, Karen, 1963-
Hello-- hello : a romantic satire / Karen Hines.

A play.
ISBN-13: 978-1-55245-171-7
ISBN-10: 1-55245-171-2

I. Title.

PS8615.I44H44 2006 C812'.6 C2006-901686-0

for Blake

We live in a dream world. With a small, rational part of the brain, we recognise that our existence is governed by material realities, and that, as those realities change, so will our lives. But underlying this awareness is the deep semi-consciousness that absorbs the moment in which we live, then generalises it, projecting our future lives as repeated instances of the present. This, not the superficial world of our reason, is our true reality. All that separates us from the indigenous people of Australia is that they recognise this and we do not.

Our dreaming will, as it has begun to do already, destroy the conditions necessary for human life on Earth. Were we governed by reason, we would be on the barricades today, dragging the drivers of Range Rovers and Nissan Patrols out of their seats, occupying and shutting down the coal-burning power stations, bursting in upon the Blairs' retreat from reality in Barbados and demanding a reversal of economic life as dramatic as the one we bore when we went to war with Hitler.

George Monbiot
The Guardian, August 12, 2003

Introduction

Hello … Hello was written during the nineties, when serious cuts to spending on the environment, the public sphere and the arts were underway. The general idea was that we should adhere to more commercial models on all fronts.

My reaction, perhaps perverse, was to embrace this new order by writing a love story set in a place and time where art and commerce have finally and completely conjoined: a romantic fable for a new world. The absence of props and the near-empty set, which began as budgetary necessities, quickly became key to the play's point of view. Words were free, so I used a lot of them, and soon the spoken stage directions, with their lush descriptions of glowing snowfalls, mammoth set pieces and dancing accountants, set the stage for a piece of theatre that could both celebrate and subvert the classic styles of escapist entertainment it employed.

Despite the fact that *Hello … Hello* was riddled with romance, comedy and songs, it became increasingly clear during the very first workshop that it was not really a romantic musical comedy, and shouldn't pretend to be. Or should only pretend to be. Perhaps, we thought, it was an 'allegorical romance with songs.' Or a 'black romantic tragi-comedy.' Whatever the genre, obstacles became our compasses and limitations our guides. The ironic juxtaposition of nothingness and 'everythingness' was mined for its comedy. The romance was mined for its appeal. The darker suggestions regarding romantic love and its macrocosmic reverberations were left to seep out from between the lines.

The world has changed a lot since this play was begun, and it's changing faster and faster. The belief I had just ten years ago in the power of art to change the world is being challenged by the probability that economic progress can change it faster and more everlastingly. But, as Kalle Lasn, founder of *Adbusters* magazine, says, 'On the far side of cynicism lies freedom.' And I suppose, at its most basic level, this play is an ode to the pursuit of freedom. It is also an ode to art itself, which seems, increasingly, to be something akin to that tiny endangered frog we have all seen in *National Geographic* or *Scientific American*: the one that is tinier than a fingertip, exquisitely beautiful, morbidly fragile …

This play is an ode to that frog.

Notes

Hello … Hello is an affectionate but unforgiving meditation on escapist consumer culture and on that most escapist of entertainments, the boy-meets-girl musical. Though it is a musical piece of theatre, its production should resist classification as a traditional musical, and though the romance between the characters is very real, every similarity to actual romantic comedies should be carefully considered.

Hello … Hello is not an attack on the musical theatre form; it is a meditation on the human impulses that lie beneath that form.

Sentiment is defined by some as the absence of actual feeling. *Hello … Hello* should at all times be a-sentimental.

Characters

BEN CORDAIR, Head of Creative at Quicksilver Incorporated.
CASSANDRA, a salesgirl at The Abyss.
FEMALE CHORUS, who narrates and plays fifty-one other roles.
MALE CHORUS, who narrates and plays fifty-three other roles.

The performers who play these roles should not be cast only to type but also for their ability to parody type. Their singing and dancing skills are important, but, again, primarily insofar as they augment the performers' abilities to parody the musical form. Comedic precision and a satirical bent are, in the end, the key elements.

Chorus

The chorus in *Hello … Hello* is inspired both by kathartic Greek tragedians and by the enthusiastic hoofers in Hollywood-style musicals. Theirs is a human voice. They sympathize with

Cassandra, Ben and all of the citizens of the megalopolis, while also standing apart from them. No gladness can entice them inside the drama for long, and no catastrophe can overwhelm them. They are inquistive, engaged, intensely human creatures.

The chorus performers are required to shape-shift and to embody dozens of characters without dropping a beat; to communicate character differentiations through the tilt of a head, a slouch, a gentle lisp. For these and for other reasons, it may be helpful when staging the play to think of the chorus as creatures who occupy an existential realm somewhere between those of angels and ghosts.

Music

Hello … Hello is a musical – of sorts. It is a musical play that eschews the curiously sacred parameters of the Broadway-style musical, and instead uses music and parody in the pursuit of other, perhaps more contentious, aims. The play's songs are inspired by Hollywood musicals from the twenties and thirties, but also by cartoons from the fifties, post-Beatles pop ballads, drum and bass and long-distance savings plan commercials. By connecting some dots between twentieth-century entertainment and contemporary reality, and by lacing the play's lullabies and adagios with tunes inspired by (often deeply affecting) television commercials, the goal has been the creation of a self-consuming artifact, a musical that uses music to meditate on some of the more troubling impulses behind that most delightful of escapist forms: the musical.

The complete score of *Hello … Hello* is over a hundred pages long, and so cannot be included here in its entirety. A sampling of the songs begins on page 150; the complete score is available through Coach House Books (mail@chbooks.com or 416 979 2217).

Costumes

The performers should wear sleek, stylish outfits that are flattering yet neutral enough to allow for the transformations between the many characters they describe and embody.

Set and Props

There is no set except, perhaps, for a bed and two chairs or something that can work as both. In addition, risers, stairs and poles or cables may help the actors to render the illusions of the settings that they describe.

The only props are a tiny bassinet and a very small light source that can be palmed, then placed inside the bassinet. The rest of the props are imaginary and may be rendered through a system of gestures and movements that are simple and precise, but never slavish to the text.

Venue

An intimate venue that allows for direct eye contact between the performers and the audience is ideal.

Production History

Hello ... Hello was produced three times in Toronto between 1998 and 2003. Each production was directed by Chris Earle, with musical direction by Greg Morrison. The music was composed by Greg Morrison with song melodies by Morrison and Hines.

Hello ... Hello was first performed in 1998 in a workshop production at The SPACE in Toronto.

Ben Cordair: Steven Guy-McGrath
Cassandra: Karen Hines
Female Chorus: Teresa Pavlinek
Male Chorus: Steve Morel

The premiere was presented by Pochsy Productions at the Factory Studio Theatre, in association with Factory Theatre, in April 1999.

Ben Cordair: David Jansen
Cassandra: Karen Hines
Female Chorus: Teresa Pavlinek
Male Chorus: Steve Morel

In November 2003, *Hello ... Hello* was presented by the Tarragon Theatre.

Ben Cordair: Peter Oldring
Cassandra: Karen Hines
Female Chorus: Aurora Browne
Male Chorus: Steve Morel

Hello … Hello

Twilight in the Megalopolis

Soft, flattering lights come up on a tall, beautiful woman, the FEMALE CHORUS, wearing a stylish ensemble. She is exquisitely made-up – her lips red, her cheeks pale, her lashes thick. She looks like an angel in Calvin Klein. She speaks directly to the audience.

FEMALE CHORUS: In a sparkling city on a spinning green globe in the centre of the universe, it is nearly twilight. Office buildings, banks and a trillion gleaming billboards thrust high up into the sky. The streets are empty, as everyone is at work in this thriving megalopolis.

Lights up on a tall man, the MALE CHORUS, standing nearby. He is at least as beautiful as the Female Chorus. His outfit is possibly more stylish. He admires the woman for a moment, then speaks directly to the audience.

MALE CHORUS: Though the sun itself has slipped behind the jagged megalopolitan horizon, its reflections still hover in the mirrored windows of the highest office towers.

FEMALE CHORUS: And before night falls, the shimmering reproductions will lure a thousand sparrows and swallows toward pinker, more glimmering skies …

MALE CHORUS: … then surely and swiftly …

BOTH: … take their breath away.

The Chorus looks up.
sfx: small birds plummeting through the air.
The Chorus watches the fall. They look at each other, then both look at the audience. They sigh.

Music in: 'Megalopica,' a pulsing ur-urban theme. The Chorus clears to stage left and right as lights come up on BEN and CASSANDRA draped gorgeously across stairs. They are gazing at one another with open adoration.

BEN: Six o'clock.

CASSANDRA: Sharp.

Ben and Cassandra turn to the audience.

BEN: In a sparkling city on a spinning green globe, office workers, lawyers and switchboard operators spill from the buildings and onto the street, where they mill beneath the glowing sky.

Ben and Cassandra walk down toward the Chorus.

CASSANDRA: Sales clerks, executives and manicurists descend from the towers, rise up from the underground and join the swelling stream of humanity that fills the city streets with living motion.

BOY: The sophistication with which the people navigate their interweaving paths does little to obscure the untamed life force that gushes through their wild hearts and courses through their red and blue and pulsing veins.

All four performers form a line across centre stage, in the manner of Teatro en Atril. *Though they remain centre stage as a group, each performer begins to embody the characters he or she describes. They enjoy increasing contact with one another over the course of the scene. The musical pulse quickens. Performers' gestures are descriptive, economical. Their movements are precise.*

MALE CHORUS: In the grand arched doorway of a thriving business firm, a cluster of telemarketers gathers and peers out at the beautiful sky.

BEN (AS TELEMARKETER 1): Look at the sky!

MALE CHORUS (AS TELEMARKETER 2): So blue!

CASSANDRA (AS TELEMARKETER 3): Look at the sky!

BEN (AS TELEMARKETER 1): So green!

MALE CHORUS (AS TELEMARKETER 2): Look at the sky!

CASSANDRA (AS TELEMARKETER 3): So blue!

MALE CHORUS (AS TELEMARKETER 2): So green!

ALL: It's both at once, it seems!

FEMALE CHORUS (AS TELEMARKETER 4): Has the sun set yet?

ALL: Not quite yet!

FEMALE CHORUS: The telemarketers spill onto the street, whirling and spinning beneath the blue-green sky.

BEN: Some of the people know each other.

MALE CHORUS (AS LENNY): Peggy!

FEMALE CHORUS (AS PEGGY): Lenny!

MALE CHORUS (AS LENNY): Nice to see you!

CASSANDRA: While others swirl around the gentle strangers who cross their paths.

The Female Chorus spins into Ben's arms. Their lips are very close together.

BEN (AS STRANGER 1): I beg your pardon!

FEMALE CHORUS (AS STRANGER 2): I'm all left feet!

BEN (AS STRANGER 1): Must be something in the air, it seems.

FEMALE CHORUS (AS STRANGER 2): Must be something in the breeze.

MALE CHORUS: In the darkened doorway of another thriving firm, a pride of CEOs gazes out at the beautiful sky.

CASSANDRA (AS CEO 1): Look at the sky!

FEMALE CHORUS (AS CEO 2): It's purple!

BEN (AS CEO 3): Look at the sky!

CASSANDRA (AS CEO 1): It's lime!

FEMALE CHORUS (AS CEO 2): Look at the sky!

BEN (AS CEO 3): Look at the sky!

ALL: It's both at the same time!

MALE CHORUS (AS CEO 4): Has the sun set?

ALL: Not quite yet!

CASSANDRA: They scatter and *jeté* down the street.

FEMALE CHORUS: High up on a scaffolding, two workers are busy erecting a billboard. Emerging from the scattered jigsaw of squares and ziggurats is a fractured image whose truth and beauty are known only to the workers, but whose mystery holds the attention of a thousand eyes for blocks around.

BEN (AS JOHN): *(softly, looking down)* Look at them, Mike. They want to see the picture.

MALE CHORUS (AS MIKE): Only so fast we can go, John.

JOHN: But look at them. Their faces tilted up like that. I can almost see their eyes!

MIKE: Their eyes?

JOHN: Their eyes ...

MIKE: *(gently)* Don't look down any more, John. It'll be all right.

JOHN: They long to be what dreams are made of ...

MIKE: Come on, John. Don't look down now. We've got work to do.

JOHN: Sorry, Mike. I don't know what's gotten into me.

MIKE: That's all right, John. You're only being human.

John goes back to work. Mike sneaks a look at their eyes.

BEN: In another darkened doorway, an anguish of accountants gathers. Pale fingers twitch furiously over phantom adding machines, working equations that yet tangle their minds.

CASSANDRA (AS ACCOUNTANT 1): Has the sun set yet?

FEMALE CHORUS, MALE CHORUS AND BEN (AS ACCOUNTANTS 2, 3 AND 4): Shhhh.

MALE CHORUS: There is a magical transformation of the light as the sunset turns to twilight.

Music swells. Lights shift.

ALL: Look at the sky!

FEMALE CHORUS (AS ACCOUNTANT 2): It's indigo!

MALE CHORUS (AS ACCOUNTANT 3): It's primrose!

CASSANDRA (AS ACCOUNTANT 1): It's chartreuse!

ALL: It's all of those!

FEMALE CHORUS: The accountants toss their visors to the wind and do a mad ecstatic dance, leaping wildly over moving cars and twirling on the lips of dumpsters – the savage twisting polka with which they greet the falling of the night.

All dance in place: a slow-motion ecstasy twist.
Music transition: trippy.

CASSANDRA: Now the cinemas throw open their doors to swallow the snaking queues that yearn to bathe their eyes with brilliant beauty and their minds with simple truths.

MALE CHORUS (AS TIMID MOVIEGOER): Are you in line?

CASSANDRA, BEN AND FEMALE CHORUS: (*in rapturous anticipation*) Oh, yes!

BEN: The cocktail lounges turn on their neon signs, inviting the beautiful creatures into their pleasure dens, wherein strange scents and stranger music offer the promise of romantic transcendence.

CASSANDRA: In the shadows outside, a young newlywed couple stands locked in a delicate embrace. A psychic eddy threatens to furrow the bride's pale brow and to dim the sparkle in her beautiful eyes.

MALE CHORUS (AS NEWLYWED MAN): What's the matter, baby?

FEMALE CHORUS (AS NEWLYWED WOMAN): I don't know. I just feel so sad.

BEN: He turns her toward the gleaming plate glass window of the thriving banking institution in front of which they stand.

NEWLYWED MAN: Look in that window. What do you see?

NEWLYWED WOMAN: I see ... myself.

NEWLYWED MAN: No. Look further. Look through that window.

CASSANDRA: Through the gleaming bank window, there is an enormous poster in which a rosy-cheeked woman stands in a brilliant white kitchen, gazing out over a pie that is cooling on the windowsill. Beyond the windowsill lie an emerald-green field, a dog, a horse and a man.

NEWLYWED MAN: Now what do you see?

NEWLYWED WOMAN: I see a vista fathomless and vast …

NEWLYWED MAN: Yes?

NEWLYWED WOMAN: I see possibility more vibrant than all my dreams …

NEWLYWED MAN: Yes?

NEWLYWED WOMAN: I see the future. And it's bright, Tyley!

NEWLYWED MAN: Yes! Very bright!

They kiss.

BEN: From inside the bank, the financial services manager gazes out at the young newlyweds on the sidewalk and wipes a single tear from his cheek. He pulls out his cellphone and hits a key.

MALE CHORUS (AS MANAGER): (*into cellphone*) Hi there, precious. I'm on my way.

FEMALE CHORUS (AS WIFE): (*into phone*) Hurry home, love. Supper's on the stove.

CASSANDRA: (*leaning in toward Male Chorus's phone*) Through the cellphone receiver, we hear a horse's neigh, a dog's bark and the unmistakable sound of a pie sliding onto a windowsill.

BEN: The bank manager locks the door, leaps over a dumpster, bounds past the dancing accountants and somersaults through the open sunroof of his gleaming car.

MALE CHORUS: Two teenage girls wander slowly down the street. The thin fabric of their stylish ensembles clings to their youthful forms in a way that is alluring, though totally unconscious on their part.

FEMALE CHORUS (AS TEENAGE GIRL 1): What's the matter, Lauren?

CASSANDRA (AS TEENAGE GIRL 2): I don't know. I just feel funny.

TEENAGE GIRL 1: What kind of funny?

TEENAGE GIRL 2: I don't know. Must be something in the air. I'm restless in my body, and somehow I fear I'll fly away.

TEENAGE GIRL 1: Don't be frightened, Lauren. Look up there.

MALE CHORUS: High up on a scaffolding, the two billboard workers are still busy. Emerging now from the scattered jigsaw of squares and ziggurats is the fractured image of a beautiful woman in a gleaming white slip dress.

TEENAGE GIRL 1: What do you see?

TEENAGE GIRL 2: I see myself, somehow.

TEENAGE GIRL 1: Somestrangehow I see me too. Close your eyes and make a wish.

BEN: The girls close their thick-lashed eyes ...

MALE CHORUS: ... and dream of magic, love and the world's deepest mysteries of creation.

Lighting transition: twilight to cool night.
sfx: a chirping sparrow.

MALE CHORUS: High up in the office towers, glittering windows signal to the sky that on this pale night, as on all the other nights, the stars above need not shine.

FEMALE CHORUS: And on this beautiful night, each and every citizen moves inexplicably, inexorably and ingeniously away from the sucking void that cries out their name.

Cassandra breaks away and gazes out over the audience, en pose.

MALE CHORUS: That is, each and every citizen but one.

Snow

Music in: 'Snow Song.' Very sweet, very sad. Like a Disney lament. There is a moment of dispersal, as the other performers go left and right. They watch Cassandra. She sings.

CASSANDRA:

Seems the sky has fallen down,
Stars have tumbled to the ground.
I'd make a wish
'Cept I'm bidding wishing toodle-oo.
I've only got one wish,
And it's never coming true … oo-oooh.

'Snow Song' continues under the following narration. At times, Cassandra hums along. She walks.

MALE CHORUS: A girl drifts along the street, gliding over the glimmering sewer grates with unseeing eyes. She swings a bouquet of sapphire-blue daisies by her side.

FEMALE CHORUS: A boy stands at the box office of a movie theatre with a hundred-dollar bill in his hand.

Ben embodies the movie-lineup boy.

FEMALE CHORUS: The bill is whisked away by a little gust of wind caused by a tiny vortex created by the motion of the girl.

sfx: pretty vortex.
Ben sees Cassandra.

CHORUS: The boy follows the bill.

Lighting grows cooler.

MALE CHORUS: Snow falls.

FEMALE CHORUS: The girl walks into a graveyard that has lots of graves in it.

MALE CHORUS: All the stones are engraved 'Rest in Peace.'

FEMALE CHORUS: Some do, some don't.

MALE CHORUS: The girl stares up at the pale green sky and extends her arms to catch the falling snow.

FEMALE CHORUS: In the blackness of the graveyard, a single star is visible in the sky.

Cassandra gasps.

MALE CHORUS: It falls.

CASSANDRA: (*disappointed*) Oh. (*She sings.)*
I'd wish the world's darkest mystery
Would come up clear:
Why it's the sparkling things
That always disappear.

FEMALE CHORUS: The girl stares at the snowflakes she has caught.

Cassandra brings her hands toward her face.

MALE CHORUS: They melt on her fingers.

CASSANDRA: (*very disappointed*) Oh!

But that'd be like wishing
That two and two made five.
That'd be like wishing
That you, my dear, were still alive.
My sweetie-pie.

CASSANDRA: Hello, pet. (*She kneels.*) I brought you some flowers. I don't think their colour is natural. I think it was done to them. But here. I'm dedicating them to you. (*She places the flowers on the ground.*)

I'm trying to carry on, love. Like you said. Trying to ... hang on. Some days, though, I just don't seem to have the heart for it. (*hushed*) Some days I guess I wish you'd left a drop for me.

She sings.

Only you will ever be my honey lamb.
Only you, but there you are and here I am.
And my wish will never come true,
So I'll keep one of my feet
In the grave with you,
My sweetie-pie.

She stands.

In the gra-a-ave
With yo-o-ou.

FEMALE CHORUS: The girl digs the sole of one shoe deep into the cold earth.

sfx: digging sole.

MALE CHORUS: A hundred-dollar bill skitters across the grave.

sfx: skittering bill.

The girl looks up and into the shining eyes of the movie-lineup boy.

Music out.

FEMALE CHORUS: They just stay like that for a minute.

Pause.

BEN: Hello.

Pause.

CASSANDRA: Hello ...

FEMALE CHORUS: The girl instinctively reaches for her key, as a weapon, but drops it –

CASSANDRA: Oh!

FEMALE CHORUS: – and stares, unseeing, into the snow.

CASSANDRA: Oh, dear. I dropped my key. I was reaching for it as ... as a ... a ... (*She makes a little stabbing motion.*)

BEN: Weapon?

CASSANDRA: Yes! But then I dropped it in the snow.

BEN: I'll help you find it.

CASSANDRA: No!

BEN: You don't have to be afraid of me.

CASSANDRA: (*genuinely*) That's what they all say.

BEN: (*even more genuinely*) I'm sorry.

Pause.

BEN: Do you mind my asking what you're doing here? In the graveyard? So late at night?

CASSANDRA: Well, yes! Unless you own this graveyard, I don't think that's any of your … your … (*She acts out a financial transaction of some sort.)*

BEN: … business?

CASSANDRA: Yes!

BEN: Forgive me.

Little pause.

FEMALE CHORUS: She does.

Pause.

CASSANDRA: I was … *(She searches.)*

BEN: … grieving?

CASSANDRA: Yes. Yes, I was weeping over someone I once … (*She touches her heart.*)

BEN: … loved?

CASSANDRA: (*softly, wide-eyed, wondering how he could know*) Why … yes.

BEN: Well, I can understand that.

CASSANDRA: Can you?

BEN: Oh yes.

MALE CHORUS: They pause. They watch each other breathe for a moment.

Pause.

CASSANDRA: Do you mind my asking what you're doing here? In this graveyard? So late at night?

BEN: I've been coming here since my girl died.

CASSANDRA: Your daughter?

BEN: No, no. I mean my …

CASSANDRA: … girlfriend.

BEN: (*wondering how she could know*) Yes. We were to have been married. But she …

CASSANDRA: (*very delicately*) … died.

MALE CHORUS: The boy just stares at the girl as though she is Einstein.

BEN: So I guess you could say I've done a fair bit of grieving here myself.

CASSANDRA: Well, I can understand that.

BEN: Can you?

CASSANDRA: Oh yes.

Pause.

FEMALE CHORUS: The boy spies the key at the girl's feet and plucks it from the snow.

BEN: Here. Your key.

CASSANDRA: Thank you.

There is a moment of stillness as, in the passing of the key, their hands touch. Their hands part.

BEN: Is this your husband?

CASSANDRA: Yes. Well, no. I mean ... We never actually ... We were ... (*She searches, then makes a little diving motion.*)

BEN: Engaged?

CASSANDRA: Yes. Yes, we had a few glorious years of the most outrageous joy. But now I will never know joy again. Never again will I see my companion in this life. Which is to say ...

BOTH: ... never.

Cassandra's jaw drops, delicately. She turns toward Ben.

CASSANDRA: Say! How come we seem to know exactly what the other one's going to say even before we –

BEN: – say it?

CASSANDRA: Yes!

BEN: Because we're the same, you and me.

CASSANDRA: Yes, I can see that. And somehow, that makes me feel just a little –

BEN: – better?

CASSANDRA: Yes.

Music in: 'The Shiny Ball Song.' A bright little number. Cassandra and Ben sing. Each time one finishes the other's sentence, both are thrilled and delighted.

CASSANDRA:

Under every rock there is a … a …

BEN:

Ladybug.

They smile.

BEN:

Inside every can of worms there lies …

CASSANDRA:

A pearl.
In the midst of any mess there is a
Shi –

BEN:

– ny

BOTH:

Ball!
I'm so glad that you're the same as me.

Cassandra and Ben dance a little soft-shoe number on the graves.

BEN:

Deep in every kettle of fish there is a –

CASSANDRA:

Pie!
In the middle of any nasty jam there's –

BEN:

Kittens.

CASSANDRA:

Purrrr!

BOTH:

In the midst of any mess there is a
Shi-i-i-ny ba-a-all!

BEN:

I'm so glad that you're the same as –

CASSANDRA:

I'm so glad that you're the same as –

BOTH:

I'm so glad that you're the same as –
Me-e-e-e-e.

Ben and Cassandra dance a little more, then twirl into one another. Music out.

FEMALE CHORUS: The boy and girl stand with their lips very close together. Snow falls again.

CASSANDRA: Well, good night. And ... thank you.

Cassandra starts to walk away.

BEN: Would you ... Would you like me to walk you home?

CASSANDRA: Um ...

She looks at him.

CASSANDRA: Yes.

She looks at his coat.

CASSANDRA: And ... could I please have your coat?

BEN: Of course.

CASSANDRA: I didn't read the weather report this morning. I didn't realize the temperature was going to plummet by forty-five degrees in one afternoon.

BEN: Yes, that's been happening a lot lately.

CASSANDRA: Yes, it has. And my coat is rather thin.

BEN: (*placing his coat on her shoulders*) I guess that's why you're shivering.

CASSANDRA: Yes. *(She touches his coat. She drops her eyes.)* I guess that's why ...

They begin to exit.

FEMALE CHORUS: The girl stops, looks back at the grave, starts to blow a kiss, redirects it to the right grave and turns to leave.

Ben snatches the kiss mid-air and, unbeknownst to Cassandra, slips it into his breast pocket.
sfx: kiss-snatch.

Lie Down on Me

Music in: 'Only You' variations, sweet, but with the occasional discord.

FEMALE CHORUS: The boy walks the girl home from the graveyard. He does not offer her his arm, as both his arms are wrapped around himself. He shivers happily in the cold night air.

MALE CHORUS: They pass the young newlywed couple, who are falling asleep in each other's arms on a shadowy park bench. They whisper into each other's ears and paint brilliant pictures in each other's minds of emerald fields and financial plans that soothe each other painless.

FEMALE CHORUS: On a freeway, miles away, the bank manager speaks love words into his phone:

MALE CHORUS (AS BANK MANAGER): That's right, honey. The world is our oyster. And you, my sweet, are the ruby nestled within.

FEMALE CHORUS (AS WIFE): Hurry home, love. Supper's almost done.

MALE CHORUS: On the stone steps of her apartment building, the girl and the boy stand at a slight distance from one another.

Music out.

CASSANDRA: Thank you. For walking me home.

BEN: The pleasure was all mine.

CASSANDRA: (*sincerely*) No. It wasn't. It was my pleasure, too.

Pause.

BEN: Well ... good night.

CASSANDRA: Good night.

Ben shivers.

CASSANDRA: Oh! (*She returns his coat.*) And ... thank you.

Cassandra turns to leave.

MALE CHORUS: A little clump of graveyard dirt tumbles from the sole of the girl's shoe.

CASSANDRA: Oh ...

FEMALE CHORUS: A light breeze blows.

CASSANDRA: Oh, dear ... (*She swoons.*)

BEN: What's the matter?

CASSANDRA: Nothing. It's nothing. (*She holds on to a post.*)

BEN: Something's the matter.

CASSNADRA: It's nothing. Don't worry. Just open my door, please. I can't find my key.

BEN: It's inside your pocket.

CASSANDRA: My hands. I can't.

BEN: You'd like me to get it?

CASSANDRA: Please get me my key.

FEMALE CHORUS: The wind blows harder.

CASSANDRA: Oh, dear. The sky is falling.

BEN: The sky is falling?

CASSANDRA: The clouds are all falling!

BEN: Just hold still and I'll get you your key.

CASSANDRA: (*terrified*) Hold me down. I'm flying away.

BEN: You must have a fever.

CASSANDRA: I'm cold as ice.

BEN: Your eyes are so bright.

CASSANDRA: My eyes see both ways.

BEN: I'll get you a doctor.

CASSANDRA: Just hold me down!

BEN: Just hold my arms.

CASSANDRA: I'm losing ground.

BEN: You'll be all right!

CASSANDRA: I'm flying off …

BEN: Just hold my arms!

CASSANDRA: The earth!

sfx: ugly vortex.

CASSANDRA: LIE DOWN ON ME!

Ben leaps on top of Cassandra.

MALE CHORUS: Immediately, the wind dies down. It is replaced by gentle, tinkly, happy music. The boy and girl lie in a heap for a moment, perfectly still. Their lips are very close together.

BEN: Are you all right?

CASSANDRA: (*totally back to normal*) Yes. Thank you.

They disentangle themselves and he helps her to stand.

CASSANDRA: Thank you.

She brushes herself off and pats her crazed hair down.

CASSANDRA: (*genuinely*) Thank you.

BEN: Will you be all right?

CASSANDRA: No. Really. It happens all the time.

Pause.

BEN: Can I call on you sometime?

CASSANDRA: Um … (*She looks at him.*) No.

BEN: Oh.

He looks at her.

CASSANDRA: But you could visit me at work.

BEN: Where do you work?

CASSANDRA: At that clothing store. Just down the street. We passed it just now. The Abyss.

BEN: Oh. The Abyss.

CASSANDRA: Yes. (*big Chiclet smile*) I'm a salesgirl.

She goes to leave.

BEN: What's your name?

CASSANDRA: Cassandra. And you are … ?

BEN: Ben.

Pause.

CASSANDRA: Good night, Ben. (*She touches the flesh of his cheek.*) It was lovely to meet you.

She stays like that for a minute.

FEMALE CHORUS: Cassandra turns and looks down, puzzled by the little clump of dirt on the steps. Then she lightly steps over it and goes inside.

MALE CHORUS: Ben just stands there for a minute. Then he races down the sidewalk, swinging himself wildly around lamp-posts and kicking at snow drifts.

Music in: 'More Snow.' Very sweet, much less sad.

CHORUS:

Ah ah, oh ah ah, oh … (*continues through song*)

BEN AND CASSANDRA:

Seems the sky is falling down,
Stars are tumbling all around.

MALE CHORUS: Now, the cocktail lounges empty themselves of their patrons, who have been transformed this evening by the power of each other's kind attention and who leave the clubs more beautiful, even, than when they arrived.

BEN AND CASSANDRA:

I'll make a wish,
And a little psychic switcheroo.

FEMALE CHORUS: Audiences spill from the movie houses – their stained unconsciouses collectively cleansed – and wander back out into the night reborn, yearning to dive again into the riddles of humanity and to feel the current of that endless stream tickle at their wills.

ALL:

And when all those stars
Have fallen through
The blackness of the sky,

BEN AND CASSANDRA:

And hissed their final sigh –

The Chorus sighs in celestial harmony.

BEN AND CASSANDRA:

Lucky me!

ALL:

Seems my wish
Can't help but come true.

MALE CHORUS: High up on the scaffolding, the billboard workers complete their sacred task. The billboard is enormous and lit by a hundred lights. In a black and white photograph, a beautiful girl sits on a white chair.

FEMALE CHORUS: She wears a white slip dress, so ethereal a harsh word would send it flying away.

The Female Chorus embodies the girl in the billboard.

MALE CHORUS: Her head is tilted, and she gazes at the razor blade she holds poised over her wrist. Her elbows are clenched to her sides, causing her breasts to squeeze together. She gently bites her full lower lip. The caption of the billboard reads:

FEMALE CHORUS: (*wispily*) Don't ruin the dress.

MALE CHORUS: In the foreground, big in the frame …

Music out.

… there is a shiny ball.

Music in again.

ALL: (*singing*)

Can't help but come true …

FEMALE CHORUS: The lights in the towers go out one by one, and as they do, the falling snowflakes glow a pale, acid yellow.

MALE CHORUS: And the ghosts of a hundred thousand swallows fly away into the night.

sfx: flying swallow souls.
All watch the swallow souls soar up. Music out.

The Abyss

MALE CHORUS: Morning.

Music under: a sparkly morning capriccio.
Lights surge dramatically from midnight hues to blinding daylight. Ben and Cassandra leave the stage. The Chorus steps to centre, their mood effervescent.

MALE CHORUS: Overnight, the temperature has soared again, and a warm shower spills from the heavens above, sparkling in the achingly brilliant sunshine.

FEMALE CHORUS: Gushing streams of shimmering foam slide along the boulevards and down the sewer grates, swirling around the ankles of the beautiful citizens who dart from subway to office building until the streets are empty.

MALE CHORUS: Empty, save for the snaking lineup of humanity that slithers along the sidewalk and up to the faux-marble portal ... to The Abyss.

Cassandra rushes into place wearing a new outfit. The music follows her as she speaks in time.

CASSANDRA:

Good morning, gentle ladies and men,
And welcome to The Abyss.
I greet you, delighted to meet you,
On a beautiful day such as this.

'Cuz you are the reason for why I am here.
If you weren't, I wouldn't be too.
I've been carefully trained
To unlock psychic chains,
Help you realize
Your vision
(*singing*) Of yo-o-o-ou.

FEMALE CHORUS: The patrons descend the faux-marble steps, blinking into the emptiness of The Abyss.

MALE CHORUS: But as the doors swing shut, the blackness parts like the sea.

FEMALE CHORUS: Faux-mahogany tables descend from above, piled with sweaters and bright cotton Ts.

MALE CHORUS: Towering shelves roll into the room and, with a flick of a switch, spring to life in a snakes-and-ladders dance of plenty.

Music swells, the tempo kicks in and Cassandra sings 'The Abyss,' a rococo extravaganza.

CASSANDRA:

Just give your flesh to me and I'll adorn it expertly,
And doom and dread will fall in tatters to the floor.
Though the styles might seem outrageous,
Trust my promise is sagacious:
You'll feel better than you did before.

CHORUS:

When she stares into my eyes, I'm tranquilized.
My knees get melty and my eyes, they blur.
'Cuz I'm soaring o'er a chasm
That looks something like nirvana –
I'd go anywhere with her.

MALE CHORUS: A plump teenage girl guilty with truancy trembles by a bin of socks. Cassandra leads the trembling wretch into a corner flush with oblivion whites and fathomless blues and magically transforms her into a human gazelle, graceful as Cassandra herself.

CASSANDRA: *(to plump teenage girl)*
Love-ly things
Can make this bleak life worth the grieving.

FEMALE CHORUS (AS PLUMP TEENAGE GIRL):
Jing-ly rings

CASSANDRA:
Inspire the will to keep on breathing.
When your dreams
Lie dashed in shreds
Like last year's dress,
Catch the gifts
That fall to you from nothingness …

CASSANDRA AND CHORUS:
Sweaters soft as snow
Come spilling from the shelves,
Dreamier than dreams

CASSANDRA: Themselves.

All dance.

FEMALE CHORUS: And for the rest of the day, Cassandra works ceaselessly, shunning lunch and renouncing all coffee breaks, to release the damaged and the desperate who have been, until this day, imprisoned by their fashion crimes.

All dance exuberantly.

CHORUS:

When she murmurs in my ears,
I'm released of all my fears.

MALE CHORUS:

She's so dreamy,
Now my wife looks dreamy too.

CHORUS:

When she speaks so sweet and soft,
My faith returns and soars aloft.

CASSANDRA:

These cappuccino little chinos
Would look marvellous on you!

Enter Ben.

CHORUS AND CASSANDRA:

And when the blackness falls on me,

CASSANDRA:

As it will someday do,

CHORUS AND CASSANDRA:

There's nowhere I
Would rather be
Than in the bliss
Of The Abyss
With …

Music out. Cassandra spies Ben. They lock eyes.

CASSANDRA: Hello.

BEN: Hello.

Music soars back in.

CHORUS AND BEN:

When she murmurs in my ear,
I'm released of pain and fear.
It's like a thrilling chilling
Petit mort.

All gasp and quiver.

BEN:

'Cuz I heard the salesgirl sing:

Music out.

CASSANDRA: *(a cappella)*

In nothingness lies everything.

Music in.

ALL:

And I feel better than I did before!

Cassandra leaps from a high perch into the arms of the Chorus. They all twirl and spin. Ben escorts Cassandra to two chairs, centre stage, as 'The Abyss' ends with a big finish.

Angel Doll

FEMALE CHORUS: In a restaurant, on a date. A bouquet of blood-red trilliums adorns the table.

MALE CHORUS: Ben and Cassandra have ordered cod. The waiter has informed them that the restaurant has been out of cod for twenty-seven years.

CASSANDRA: (*disappointed*) Ohhh …

MALE CHORUS: They order zebra mussels instead, and pick quivering beads of mercury from their dinners as they chat.

CASSANDRA: And what do you do? For a living?

BEN: Well, that's difficult to say, really. I work for a company. That sells things to people. That markets things.

CASSANDRA: What kind of things?

BEN: All sorts of things, really. Things that … people want. That people need. Things that make them feel …

CASSANDRA: … better?

BEN: (*little pause*) Yes.

CASSANDRA: And what do you do? At the company?

BEN: I'm head of Creative.

CASSANDRA: (*puzzled)* Creative … ?

BEN: Yes.

CASSANDRA: Oh. *(She doesn't actually get it.)*

Pause.

BEN: You were like a dream today.

CASSANDRA: I beg your pardon?

BEN: At your work. Today. With the people. You were … like a dream. Is that what you're really like? Dreamy?

CASSANDRA: Um … yes. (*pause*) What is it called? Your company.

BEN: Quicksilver Incorporated.

CASSANDRA: Meaning … ?

BEN: (*puzzled*) Meaning?

CASSANDRA: Meaning. What does it mean?

BEN: Quicksilver?

CASSANDRA: Yes.

BEN: Well, I never really thought about it.

CASSANDRA: Oh.

Pause.

BEN: You understood them.

CASSANDRA: Whom?

BEN: The people … whom you were serving. You understood them, and they were transformed.

CASSANDRA: Oh, I don't understand them.

BEN: You're a deep girl, aren't you?

CASSANDRA: I'm just a cipher.

BEN: I beg your pardon?

CASSANDRA: (*covering*) I said … I'm just a salesgirl.

BEN: (*gravely*) A deep salesgirl.

CASSANDRA: (*lightly*) Oh, I just like the clothes.

Pause.

BEN: I brought you a gift, if you don't mind.

CASSANDRA: You shouldn't have.

BEN: It's nothing, really. Go on, open it.

MALE CHORUS: Cassandra unwraps the beautifully wrapped package. Inside there is a beautiful angel doll, all white and gold and pearly. Cassandra is dumbfounded.

BEN: Go on, pull the string.

FEMALE CHORUS: She does. The angel doll sings.

MALE CHORUS (AS DOLL): (*singing*)
Heaven, I'm in heaven,
And my heart beats so that I can hardly …

BEN: It's part of a set. The others sing in harmony. There are three in all: three-part harmony.

During the following exchange, Ben does not take his eyes from Cassandra, who does not take her eyes from the angel doll.

CASSANDRA: Where on earth did you get such a thing?

BEN: I … I made it.

CASSANDRA: You mean your company?

BEN: Well, no. These are ... just sort of a hobby.

CASSANDRA: *You* made this?

BEN: Well, yes.

CASSANDRA: (*little gasp*) But this is ... like ... art. (*pause*) It's terribly beautiful.

Ben sighs with relief.

BEN: Twist off its head. Go on. Twist it off.

Cassandra is horrified.

BEN: Go on.

CASSANDRA: No! No, I couldn't possibly *twist off* –

BEN: (*gently taking the doll*) That's okay. Allow me.

MALE CHORUS: Ben twists off the angel doll's head and hands it to Cassandra.

BEN: Go on, put some on. It's perfume.

FEMALE CHORUS: She dabs on some perfume, and citrus, musk and the tears of wild things rise up from her pulsing wrists.

BEN: It had you written all over it.

CASSANDRA: Well, there you're wrong. Though I wish it were true.

MALE CHORUS: Cassandra replaces the angel's head. It faces backward on its body. Neither of them seems to notice or to care.

BEN: I've been making them for years, actually. Dolls. Mugs. Night lights.

CASSANDRA: For the children.

BEN: Yes. In the night. I thought about trying to sell them but … but …

CASSANDRA: But what?

BEN: I just didn't think angels would sell. I couldn't imagine that anyone could want that which is ephemeral – *spiritual* – reduced to plaster and paint. That they could bear to dribble coffee down the faces of angels. I was afraid I might be accused of a lack of grace.

CASSANDRA: (*reassuringly*) But this is a graceless time.

BEN: (*doubtful*) Aw, I dunno …

CASSANDRA: I think you should have more confidence in yourself. (*encouraging*) There are a lot of very hopeless people out there.

BEN: (*hopefully*) You think so?

CASSANDRA: (*big smile*) They're everywhere!

FEMALE CHORUS: Cassandra gazes at the angel doll's head sitting backward on its body and sniffs the perfume on her wrist.

CASSANDRA: (*genuinely moved*) It's beautiful. It's the most terribly beautiful thing I think I ever saw.

Ben gazes at Cassandra as she gazes at the doll.

MALE CHORUS: The waiter arrives with the cheque.

BEN: (*hand on his wallet*) Oh, please. Allow me.

CASSANDRA: (*opening her purse*) No, don't be silly.

BEN: No, really. (*He takes the cheque.*) I have more money than you.

CASSANDRA: Oh. (*She closes her purse.*) Yes. (*She puts her purse away.*) Yes, you do. (*She blushes, looks away, then whispers.*) Lucky me.

FEMALE CHORUS: The waiter removes their dinner plates. A single bead of mercury falls to the floor, rolls toward the door, changes its shape a hundred times, then bursts apart into a thousand points of light.

Walking Home

FEMALE CHORUS: Ben and Cassandra walk along arm in arm. Though it is only February, a summer rain falls from the sky.

MALE CHORUS: They walk and walk, stepping lightly over the sparrows and swallows who rest peacefully on the ground beneath their feet.

FEMALE CHORUS: They walk until they reach the graveyard gates. They stop.

BEN: Would you like to have my coat again?

CASSANDRA: No, not tonight.

BEN: Would you like me to walk you home again?

CASSANDRA: No, that's all right.

MALE CHORUS: A light breeze blows.

BEN: What would you like?

CASSANDRA: I'll just find my key … (*She looks at her hands.*)

FEMALE CHORUS: A little clump of earth tumbles from beneath Cassandra's nails.

BEN: (*tenderly*) Tell me what you'd like.

FEMALE CHORUS: The moonlight glints on her dead lover's gravestone.

BEN: (*whispering*) Tell me what you need.

MALE CHORUS: A gust of wind blows her hair across her face.

CASSANDRA: Brush my hair, please, from my eyes.

BEN: Anything.

FEMALE CHORUS: He does. Wind blows harder.

CASSANDRA: Bend your ear to hear my sigh.

BEN: Anything.

MALE CHORUS: He does. Wind blows madly.

CASSANDRA: Kiss my lips so I don't cry.

BEN: Anything.

FEMALE CHORUS: He does.

CASSANDRA: (*whispering*) Lie down on me …

The Male Chorus embodies the man on the billboard as the following description progresses.

MALE CHORUS: High above them, there is a new and gleaming billboard. In a black and white photograph a hundred feet wide, a man in button-fly boxer briefs stands leaning against an exterior warehouse wall. His stomach could wash the laundry of the world.

FEMALE CHORUS: His face is streaked with tears. He eyes the asphalt six storeys below him. In the foreground, big in the frame, there is a shiny ball.

MALE CHORUS: The caption of the billboard reads: Live fast dot dot dot ...

Beat.

MALE CHORUS: Ben's place.

Music in: 'Consummation.' Seductive, propulsive.

Consummation

FEMALE CHORUS: The place is enormous and glimmering with soft and very flattering lighting. In a stunning display of radical *feng shui*, the only piece of furniture is a bed. A French door leads to a balcony. Cassandra moves through the beautiful space in wonder and in awe.

MALE CHORUS: As if he knew this would be the night, Ben has filled the room with thick scented candles and fresh-cut forget-me-nots.

CASSANDRA: Poppies!

BEN: (*politely*) Yes. They are.

FEMALE CHORUS: Cassandra touches a single forget-me-not, and all of its petals spiral to the floor.

CASSANDRA: Ooopsy daisy.

Music swells. The Chorus strikes alluring poses.

CHORUS: (*singing*)

Look how bright his thick-lashed eyes are.
Look at how his white teeth gleam.
Watch his hair shine in the light
Each time he moves, each time he breathes.

MALE CHORUS: Ben pulls an icy bottle of vodka from a silver bucket.

BEN: Would you like a martini?

CASSANDRA: Oh. No, thank you. I'm already a little tipsy.

BEN: It's Unequivocal.

CASSANDRA: Oh. Well, then.

For the rest of the scene, until their first embrace, Ben and Cassandra circle one another and drift around the room. The Chorus shadows them, but where Ben and Cassandra are elegant and restrained, the Chorus dances a slow-mo go-go erotic travelling dance.

CHORUS:

Look how bright her healthy skin glows,
Like a beacon in the death
Of night, and watch her living flesh move,
Every time she takes a breath.

FEMALE CHORUS: Ben notices as Cassandra's cardigan comes undone, falls from her pale shoulders, slides down her pale arms and onto the floor.

Cassandra flutters her lashes.

MALE CHORUS: She's not even conscious of it.

CHORUS:

Touch me, baby,
Touch me slowly,
Touch me, honey,
Make me sigh.
Touch me quick,
Before it's too late,
Touch me now
So I don't cry.

MALE CHORUS: Cassandra goes to the French doors, which swing open in response to the slight breeze her motion has created. She steps out on to the balcony and finds before her a perfect view of the graveyard. The temperature has plummeted by thirty-two degrees, and sparkling icicles now hang from the graveyard trees.

BEN: You're shivering.

CASSANDRA: Yes. I am.

FEMALE CHORUS: As the ice melts in their glasses, each watches as the other transforms into a creature even more impossibly beautiful than it was at the beginning of this beautiful night. If that's even possible.

MALE CHORUS: Cassandra leans over to smell another bouquet of forget-me-nots. (*She leans forward, toward him.*) Ben notices how attractive she looks when she does that.

BEN: You look very attractive when you do that.

CASSANDRA: Oh, really? (*beat*) I wasn't even conscious of it ...

Their hands touch 'accidentally.'

CHORUS:

Look how strong his gentle hands are,
Look at that forearm of his,
Which, when it's pressed against your flesh,
Looks bigger than it really is.

Smell the forest in her sable hair and
Smell her warm damp skin.
Smell how sweet and strange her breath is:
Lipstick, anguish, lust and mint.

Look once more into his piercing eyes and
Kiss his perfect brow.
Smooth his hair and stroke his mind,
And watch him lose all reason now.

Touch me, baby,
Touch me, sweetie,
Touch me soft but
Squeeze me tight.
Taste my lips, then
Bite my tongue and
Prove to me that
I'm alive.

Lights fade to black light. The rest of the scene is illuminated only by the glow of the couple's perfect white Calvin Klein underwear.

MALE CHORUS: Clothing falls to the floor, revealing the exquisite underclothing beneath.

FEMALE CHORUS: Both are moved to tears by the beauty of each other's under-apparel which, until this night, they had only ever seen in photographs … and in their dreams.

BEN AND CASSANDRA: Bless you.

FEMALE CHORUS: They begin to remove the underclothing.

BEN AND CASSANDRA: (*whispering*) No. Please. Leave it on.

ALL:

Touch me, baby,
Touch me slowly,
Touch me low, now,
Touch me high.
Touch me quick,
Before it's too late.

CASSANDRA:

Touch me, baby,

Music out.

'Till I die.

Music in. The Chorus emits an erotic Indo-Asian Kama Sutra warble.

MALE CHORUS: Ben lies down on Cassandra, and they become entwined in a knot that will take hours to undo.

The Chorus continues to warble.

FEMALE CHORUS: Nearby, in the graveyard, six feet under the earth's surface, there is a subtle seismic shift.

MALE CHORUS: A warm wind blows. Icicles slip from the trees, plunge to the ground and silently pierce the chilly graves below.

The Chorus offers a final Kama Sutra warbling cry. The Male Chorus spins the Female Chorus into his arms. They embrace just downstage of the half-naked lovers, eclipsing them. Blackout. Ben and Cassandra leave the stage. Music out after climax.

Morning After in the Megalopolis

Lights up.

CHORUS: The morning after.

Music in: 'Quicksilver.' Like a peppy commercial jingle, very uptempo.

MALE CHORUS: High above the glistening streets, through the most brilliant gleaming windows of the tallest office tower, nestled almost in the heavens themselves, the well-dressed young employees of Quicksilver Incorporated fly about the chromatically exquisite offices in that busy, early morning way –

FEMALE CHORUS: – leaping lightly over filing cabinets and sailing down corridors on swivel chairs, their eyes shining bright as their futures.

Into telephones, very, very fast. The Chorus embodies dozens of employees.

FEMALE CHORUS (AS EMPLOYEE 1): Good Morning, Quicksilver Incorporated.

MALE CHORUS (AS EMPLOYEE 2): Good Morning, Quicksilver Incorporated.

FEMALE CHORUS (AS EMPLOYEE 1): No, I'm sorry, Mr. Cordair has yet to arrive.

MALE CHORUS (AS EMPLOYEE 2): Though we do expect him very soon.

FEMALE CHORUS (AS EMPLOYEE 1): I certainly will!

MALE CHORUS (AS EMPLOYEE 2): I certainly will!

BOTH: You have a nice day, too!

CHORUS: (*singing*)

Sparkling new appliances can
Slow the speed of racing minds.
Gleaming silver coffeepots put
Sparkles back in deadened eyes.
Oh oh oh oh oh!
Oh oh!

Music continues under the dialogue.

MALE CHORUS (AS EMPLOYEE 2): Good morning, Quicksilver Incorporated!

FEMALE CHORUS: Over by the photocopier, a cluster of copywriters jitters.

MALE CHORUS (AS COPYWRITER 1): (*whispering*) He's never late!

FEMALE CHORUS (AS COPYWRITER 2): (*whispering*) It's half past nine!

MALE CHORUS (AS COPYWRITER 1): (*nearly hysterical*) We're so behind!

FEMALE CHORUS: They scatter and cartwheel down the hall.

The Chorus scatters and cartwheels.

CHORUS:

Glowing clocks and silver boxes,
Picture frames in sets of three.
Snappy little cameras can
Capture precious memories.
Oh oh oh oh oh!

Ben bounds to stage, a little dishevelled. The Chorus gasps. Music out.

BEN: Morning, Raiff!

MALE CHORUS (AS RAIFF): Morning, Mr. Cordair!

BEN: Morning, Katie!

FEMALE CHORUS (AS KATIE): Morning, Mr. Cordair!

BEN: Messages?

CHORUS (AS RAIFF AND KATIE): Quite a few!

BEN: (*too grateful*) Bless you! Bless you! Bless you!

The Chorus gives Ben a funny look.

MALE CHORUS: Ben breezes by the latte machine and into a mahogany-panelled conference room –

FEMALE CHORUS: – where the wildly talented junior officers of –

MALE CHORUS: – Marketing –

FEMALE CHORUS: – and Sales –

MALE CHORUS: – sip steaming Americanos and grapple with the riddles of humanity.

The following exchange is very swift. The tone is one of genuine, profound concern. Skeet and Charlize stand at the window and look down. Ben hovers, for the moment, in a shadowy corner.

SKEET: We've plumbed the depths of our minds and our wills …

CHARLIZE: And our lives are yet haunted …

SKEET: Their souls – they are lonely …

CHARLIZE: I've lost my sense –

SKEET: – of what they want. (*to Ben*) Good morning, Ben.

CHARLIZE: – of what they need …

BEN: Good morning, Skeet.

SKEET: It's half past nine.

BEN: I'm late.

SKEET: We know.

CHARLIZE: It's okay, Ben.

SKEET: We're glad you're here.

CHARLIZE: I try to not look down into their eyes …

SKEET: Their eyes …

BEN: (*looking down*) Their eyes.

CHARLIZE: Don't look down now, Skeet.

SKEET: I won't. I can't.

CHARLIZE: Come on now, Skeet. Show Ben the art.

SKEET: (*coming away from the window, showing art*) We all signed off but now they say that Graphics wants to go with grey.

BEN: (*trepidatious*) The oyster-grey or pearl?

CHARLIZE: (*desolate*) With oyster-grey.

BEN: (*surprised*) Well, who's our target on this one?

CHARLIZE: It's young.

BEN: How young? Young young?

CHARLIZE: No, sir.

SKEET: Old young.

BEN: Then pearl-grey makes more sense.

SKEET AND CHARLIZE: That's what we said!

CHARLIZE: (*leaving window*) And what about the copy, Ben?

BEN: It seems a little vague, my friends.

CHARLIZE: (*crumbling*) The bad vague, not the good, right Ben?

BEN: That's right.

CHARLIZE: We know. We thought . . .

SKEET: We thought somehow that if … if in the products, in themselves, there lay a formula or pattern that we've yet to apprehend –

BEN: (*gently*) You mean the pattern of the products, or the patterns of consumption?

SKEET: Which consumption?

CHARLIZE: The good consumption.

Charlize moves back to the window.

SKEET: We thought if in the patterns of *desire,* we found a need as yet unuttered –

Skeet moves back to the window.

CHARLIZE: – that they're trying to …

SKEET: The thing is that we hear their cries …

CHARLIZE: Look at their eyes …

SKEET: We hear their psychic –

CHARLIZE: – screams.

SKEET: Look at their eyes.

CHARLIZE: If we could but transform them, then perhaps –

BEN: Transform the screams?

CHARLIZE: Transform their pain.

BEN: Transform it into ... ?

CHARLIZE: (*floundering*) Into something ... else ...

SKEET: We've lost our sense.

CHARLIZE: Of what they want.

SKEET: We're losing ground.

CHARLIZE: Of what they need.

BEN: (*gently*) Because they're restless in their bodies.

Beat. Skeet and Charlize turn from the window and face Ben.

BEN: They are restless in their bodies.

Pause.

FEMALE CHORUS: Ben gazes out the soaring windows and over the tops of the highest clouds.

BEN: (*very carefully*) I believe that in the space *between* the products there lies a truth about humanity. About what they want. What they need. That in the breaths *between* their cries there lie ... anagrams of human desire.

Now, I have had my fair share of grief in this life. And I am not impervious to sorrow. But while those all around us are haunted by despair, by the souls of the lost, the souls of the lonely, we must keep looking ahead.

We live at a juncture in time, my friends. The rules are not clear. The universe is offering itself up to us, and we are harvesting. Precious gifts.

Think vast, Charlize. Think wild, Skeet.

(*amplified, echoing*) Nothing is too wonderful to be true.

MALE CHORUS: Skeet and Charlize stare at Ben as though the music of the spheres has just spilled from his lips.

FEMALE CHORUS: Ben stares out at a herd of clouds stampeding silently by. He watches as each cloud transforms itself into a dozen shapes and sizes, and then tumbles along.

Lights shift: the stage is flooded with halogen puddles. Cassandra re-enters and stands centre stage.

MALE CHORUS: Meanwhile, blocks away, and a hundred storeys below, Cassandra hands a soft charcoal-grey sweater to a beautiful but psychically disfigured woman who tries it on and watches as the checkers of her past fuse and blur into a clean grey slate.

FEMALE CHORUS (AS PSYCHICALLY DISFIGURED WOMAN): *(to Cassandra)* Bless you.

FEMALE CHORUS: And at six o'clock sharp, one step closer to soothing the planet painless, Ben collects Cassandra from The Abyss.

Ben crosses to Cassandra. He offers her his arm, and she accepts it. Music in: 'The Abyss' reprise.

MALE CHORUS: They wander into the twilight.

CHORUS (AS ABYSS PATRONS):

When she stares into my eyes,
I'm tranquili-i-i-i-ized …

Music out.

Exes 1: Park

The Chorus lies draped across a staircase, tangled in each other's arms.

FEMALE CHORUS: Ben and Cassandra wander through a lush green park –

MALE CHORUS: – wending their way through tangles of lovers draped damply over hillocks and war memorials.

FEMALE CHORUS: They are backlit by an endless string of popcorn vendors, candy stands and souvenir stalls selling finely detailed gorilla puppets made from the sable fur of kangaroos.

BEN: What did your husband do? For a living?

CASSANDRA: Nothing. (*Pause. She corrects herself.*) He was a poet.

She shakes her head, furrows her brow and, with difficulty, locates the correct word.

He was an artist.

BEN: Ah.

CASSANDRA: Yes. (*She shakes her head.*) Well, a *sort* of an artist.

Ben looks at her quizzically. She tries to explain.

Well, he painted and he … he sang some of his … poems. Sometimes with … with things that he had painted … um … behind him.

BEN: Ah. (*He doesn't actually get it.*)

CASSANDRA: (*thinking she's getting somewhere*) And he pointed lights at himself sometimes. And the other people in the room where he was would be in darkness. Almost as though he were on television, but where the camera should be there were … well … there were people. Like a movie, only he and the audience were actually in the same …

BEN: (*tentatively*) Room?

CASSANDRA: (*thrilled*) Yes! (*quietly*) It was quite magical, really. It was quite something: the movements of the soul captured – communicated somehow – in, and through, the movements of the flesh. On the breath. And through the air. (*She shakes her head and giggles.*) It's difficult to describe. It was a physiological phenomenon, I suppose.

BEN: A kind of chemistry.

CASSANDRA: Something like that.

Pause.

BEN: How did he die?

CASSANDRA: By his own hand. Poison. Arsenic. Hemlock. Laced with morphine. For … (*Something catches in Cassandra's throat.*)

BEN: (*gently*) For the pain?

Cassandra nods.

CASSANDRA: And which he drank from a little … a sort of, um …

BEN: (*hoarse*) … locket …

Cassandra nods.

CASSANDRA: … that he had worn for months around his neck without my ever knowing what swam inside. He wore it for months. He wore it for eleven months. It … you see, it became difficult for him to do his art and … be alive.

Pause.

What was so *strange* was that he could bring so much pleasure to others – there were about twenty or thirty people who came regularly to see this … *thing* he did – that he could bring so much pleasure to others, and yet become so miserable himself.

He said, as he lay dying, he said, 'There's no money in poetry.'

Pause. The Male Chorus cocks his head. Cassandra thinks.

Or was it 'There's no poetry in money?'

Pause. She thinks again.

I don't … (*She smiles at Ben, a little embarrassed.*) I can't remember.

BEN: What was his name?

CASSANDRA: Barry. Only, when he was christened, it was spelled B-u-r-y. I believe it was always more than difficult for him to be alive.

She pauses. Ben waits. She looks him in the eye.

CASSANDRA: We had a few years of the most outrageous joy. But then, just because you were meant to be with someone …

BEN: (*gently*) … doesn't mean you can be.

MALE CHORUS: Cassandra giggles, and a flock of lovers look around to see who is crying.

CASSANDRA: Yes, I guess everybody knows that.

FEMALE CHORUS: Ben and Cassandra wander by a bed of bluebells that have been planted and cared for by the neighbourhood's gentler psychiatric patients.

CASSANDRA: Tulips!

BEN: (*kindly*) Yes. Yes, they are.

FEMALE CHORUS: Ben takes Cassandra's hand in his. She feels knuckles and bones. Her fingers trace the long curve of an ulna.

Exes 2: Boardwalk

MALE CHORUS: Ben and Cassandra wander along the boardwalk. The sounds of crashing waves and the cries of ducks are muffled slightly by the sparkling foam that shimmers in the megalopolitan glow.

FEMALE CHORUS: They nibble maraschino cherries from a striped paper cup, occasionally tossing cherries to the shiny black ducks who frolic by the water's edge.

CASSANDRA: And your girlfriend? What did she do? For a living.

BEN: She never did anything, actually. She died too young. High school.

CASSANDRA: Oh. *(softly, understanding)* Influenza?

BEN: Yes. On the night of our prom, you see, we lay down on the Astroturf of the football field … to kiss. She was shivering, and of course I hoped it was because of me, but …

CASSANDRA: *(with dread)* Yes … ?

BEN: It was a chilly night. There was dew. The next day she wasn't feeling well. Itchy and feverish. Something in the air, she thought. Something she ate. The day after that, she had lost forty-five pounds, and her skin fell from her face and hands like petals.

CASSANDRA: Yes. I remember that flu.

BEN: I took her to emergency, but there was, by that time, a long lineup of similarly afflicted people. They sent nurses in white dresses out with hot chocolate and little baggies of antibiotics.

CASSANDRA: Oh, dear.

BEN: Yes. I held her in a blanket for three days and nights while she murmured and wasted away. Then, when we were almost up to the front of the line, she woke, shuddered and whispered in my ear:

BEN AND FEMALE CHORUS: *(softly)* There, there. There are too many people in the world anyway.

FEMALE CHORUS: There, there …

BEN: And then she …

CASSANDRA: *(softly)* Yes.

Pause.

FEMALE CHORUS: Ben and Cassandra step from the boardwalk and take three steps on shaky ground. The sand gives way beneath their feet.

BEN: It was quite beautiful, though. All those people ... all those petals of skin.

MALE CHORUS: Ben tosses a maraschino cherry out to the water's edge, where it is torn to pieces by a murder of wild-eyed ducks.

CASSANDRA: What about other girls? Since then?

BEN: Oh, there haven't been any other girls, actually. I mean, not really. She was the only one, really. (*He looks at Cassandra.*) Until now.

Cassandra blushes a little.

I channelled my energies, you see. I focused on the future.

CASSANDRA: What was her name?

BEN: Forget-me-not.

Little pause.

MALE CHORUS: The lovers toss the last cherry to a solo duck who devours it whole with ravenous enthusiasm. Slick black feathers loosen from his plump duck flesh and fly away on a fierce gust of wind.

FEMALE CHORUS: Cassandra grips Ben's arm. Ben places his hand on hers, and the wind dies down. They walk along.

MALE CHORUS: At an amusement park. Ben and Cassandra stroll through the fairway sharing a glowing cone of fluorescent-yellow banana-flavoured candy floss.

FEMALE CHORUS: High above them, riders scream madly as they are spun around and whipped about in the arms of a purple cross-eyed octopus.

BEN: (*amorously*) What do you like?

CASSANDRA: What do I ... ?

BEN: What do you like? What are your hobbies? Your pastimes? Your penchants?

Cassandra giggles.

BEN: What do you dream about? What fills your mind? Your mind's eye?

Cassandra giggles.

BEN: Tell me. I want to know.

CASSANDRA: Oh!

Ben holds her steady. She grips both his arms.

BEN: What is it?

CASSANDRA: Nothing. It's nothing.

MALE CHORUS: Far across the planet, the last lucid zebra in the world succumbs to mad zebra disease and lies down on a bed of African violets. She watches in fevered wonder as a soaring snow-capped mountain transforms before her dazzled zebra eyes into a tower of snowy white diapers … and back again.

CASSANDRA: It's nothing, really. Just hold my hand.

Ben holds Cassandra's hand and turns her to him. He touches her cheek.

BEN: You're a deep girl, aren't you?

Cassandra giggles.

Deep girls picture universes.

CASSANDRA: Oh … I just decide the socks and sweaters.

MALE CHORUS: Cassandra looks away, a little embarrassed.

FEMALE CHORUS: And deep in the chambers of Ben's heart, atoms and electrons sparkle off in all directions.

They walk along.

Tunnel of Love

In darkness.

FEMALE CHORUS: In the tunnel of love. In blackness, save for the fireflies who have been farmed in captivity and who flutter all around.

lx and sfx: fluttering fireflies.

CASSANDRA: If you could change anything about yourself, what would it be?

BEN: Oh, I don't know. I'm pretty happy the way I am. The way that I am now.

CASSANDRA: But if you had to pick *something*, what would it be?

BEN: (*little pause*) I would change my eyes.

CASSANDRA: Oh! But you have such pretty eyes!

BEN: No, I mean my vision.

CASSANDRA: Oh, are you short-sighted?

BEN: Yes. Or far-sighted. Which is it when you can see up close?

CASSANDRA: Oh, I can never remember.

BEN: Neither can I. What would you change?

CASSANDRA: I would change my nose.

BEN: But you have a beautiful nose!

CASSANDRA: Oh, thank you. Well then, I would change my chin.

BEN: Your chin is perfect.

CASSANDRA: Oh, thank you! (*coyly*) Well then … (*not coyly*) I would change my mind.

Pause.

BEN: Well, that's a woman's prerogative.

CASSANDRA: (*both amused and appalled*) Oh, Ben!

MALE CHORUS: Deep inside the testes of the male fireflies float tiny molecules which, unbeknownst to the world's scientific community, contain the missing link in the cure for smallpox.

FEMALE CHORUS: Ben and Cassandra float along.

Wishing Pond

FEMALE CHORUS: At the wishing pond. Tiny goldfish nibble at the pennies that line the bottom of a little turquoise pool. The edges of the pool are trimmed with sparkling white sand as though it were a tiny sea, and the little goldfish within, tangerine whales.

BEN: And you? Have there been any other men for you? Sin–

CASSANDRA: Ye-es. There have been. But nothing ever seemed to work out. They all seemed to think that I was somehow out of their league.

BEN: Were you?

CASSANDRA: Um ... (*She thinks.*) Yes.

Cassandra smiles at Ben and takes his hand.

FEMALE CHORUS: They walk along.

MALE CHORUS: High above them, an octopus hand flies from its arm, sending the young lovers who occupy it soaring over the Ferris wheel. They land softly on the roof of a big tent and scramble down, laughing wildly and searching for coins to ride the octopus again.

FEMALE CHORUS: On a bridge. Ben and Cassandra watch couples paddling in white plastic swans along the rubber-lined rivers.

CASSANDRA: What did your girlfriend look like?

BEN: She looked like ... a deer.

CASSANDRA: A ... a dear?

BEN: Yes. A deer.

CASSANDRA: Oh, a *deer*.

BEN: Yes.

CASSANDRA: Yes, those sweet little ... (*sigh*) ... Yes, I remember deer.

FEMALE CHORUS: Cassandra watches the water flow under the bridge. A shadow crosses her face.

BEN: Penny for your thoughts?

CASSANDRA: There is a devouring blackness that has an irresistible hold on my imagination.

BEN: I – I beg your pardon?

CASSANDRA: (*covering*) I said ... I said, 'There is a wee little sweet black dress that has a sheer invisible fold making dim fashion statements!'

BEN: That's what I thought you said. Such a cryptic girl. Aren't you? A deep and cryptic girl.

CASSANDRA: Um … (*She thinks.*) Yes.

MALE CHORUS: Two swans collide and sink. The dreamy lovers who occupied them swim languorously to the river's bank.

CASSANDRA: (*whispering into Ben's ear*) Lie down on me …

Insane

FEMALE CHORUS: Ben and Cassandra drift through the door, her head resting dreamily on his chest. She carries a stuffed cross-eyed field mouse Ben has won for her at the string-pull.

MALE CHORUS: He has filled the place with fresh-cut poppies.

CASSANDRA: Forsythia! (*murmuring, admiringly*) You're gonna spoil me.

BEN: I'm gonna try.

Ben pulls her to the bed. Cassandra puzzles over something.

CASSANDRA: Be-e-n-n-n?

BEN: Yes?

CASSANDRA: (*gravely*) You said something earlier, and I can't … mmmph! (*She racks her brain.*) It was something … about … my chin.

BEN: I said it was perfect.

CASSANDRA: Oh yes! Thank you. I couldn't recall.

BEN: Not at all.

MALE CHORUS: A slow wind rattles the French doors. The poppies sway on their stems.

FEMALE CHORUS: Cassandra touches Ben's cheek, and the wind dies down.

CASSANDRA: You have such pretty eyes.

BEN: When you look into them, what do you see?

CASSANDRA: I see ... myself.

BEN: No. Look further. Look *into* them. Do you see anything?

CASSANDRA: (*quivering*) I see ... (*whispering*) I see pies ... dogs ... fields ... a horse ...

MALE CHORUS: The wind blows harder. Poppy petals tug at their stamens.

CASSANDRA: I see visions.

FEMALE CHORUS: Cassandra kisses the pulse in Ben's neck, and the wind dies down.

BEN: (*trepidatiously*) Penny for your thoughts?

CASSANDRA: (*evasively*) My mind is a tangled web.

BEN: (*amorously*) Your mind is fathomless.

CASSANDRA: (*kittenishly*) Kiss me then. Make it shallow again.

MALE CHORUS: The wind blows the French doors wide open. Poppy petals fly around the room.

FEMALE CHORUS: Ben kisses Cassandra's mind. (*He kisses her forehead.*) The wind dies down.

MALE CHORUS: And the poppy petals softly land, to a one, on the bed.

CASSANDRA: (*murmuring*) Lie down on me.

As they start to lie down, Cassandra is poked by something on the bed.

CASSANDRA: Ow!

MALE CHORUS: Cassandra discovers another beautifully wrapped package.

CASSANDRA: You shouldn't have.

MALE CHORUS: Inside is another angel doll, more beautiful, even, than the first.

FEMALE CHORUS (AS DOLL): (*singing a harmony part*)
Heaven, I'm in heaven,
And my heart beats so that I can hardly –

BEN: Bend back its spine. Go on. Bend it back.

CASSANDRA: Oh, no, I couldn't possibly –

FEMALE CHORUS: Cassandra bends back the angel doll's spine. Nestled on a crimson cushion, where the angel's diaphragm would be ... there is a diamond ring!

CASSANDRA: Oh! It's beautiful. (*very softly*) It's the most frightfully beautiful thing I think I ever saw.

Music in: 'Insane Song.' Like a pop ballad, very tender.

BEN:

Let me smooth your troubled brow
And pull the tangles from your mind,
And though I'm somewhat terrified
Of all the knots I know I'll find,
I'm sure on earth we live but once,
Before the night comes sweeping by,
So give your hand, my sweet, or else
I may not wake before I die.
Though it may seem a bit insane,
I can't help but feel a love for
Which I cannot find a name.

Ben lifts the ring from the angel's cushion and reaches out for Cassandra's hand. She closes her eyes for a second, then opens them.

CASSANDRA:

I will give the hand I gave before,
And give the one I kept myself,
To keep a grip and save my soul
From plunging in the wishing well.
For though my thoughts run round the world,
And faster than this spinning plane,
When reason reaches out for me,
It's you that calls me back again.

CASSANDRA AND BEN:

Though once I swore I'd never slip
Back in the cosmic dizzy spell,
I've slipped and fallen for you, dear,
With all my heart, my love's unquelled.

ALL:

Though it may seem a bit insane,
I can't help but feel a love for
Which I cannot find a –

Music transition: 'Consummation' reprise. Softer, slower.

CASSANDRA:

Touch me, baby,
Touch me softly,
Kiss my lips,
So I don't cry.
Touch me quick,
Before it's too late,
Touch me, baby …

ALL BUT BEN:

Till I die.

Ben slips the ring on Cassandra's finger.

FEMALE CHORUS: Through the French doors and out on the streets below, the citizens of the megalopolis wander home in that going-home kind of way. Miles away, the bank manager rubs his weary eyes and hits a pad on his cellphone, which lights his face in a ghostly glow.

MALE CHORUS (AS BANK MANAGER): Don't worry, precious, just pop it in the oven. I'll be home soon.

FEMALE CHORUS (AS WIFE): I'll be waiting, love.

MALE CHORUS: On their shadowy park bench, the newlywed couple kiss each other's freshly naked ring fingers and wipe the trouble from each other's brows.

MALE CHORUS (AS NEWLYWED MAN): Don't worry, sweetie, we'll buy them back someday.

Cassandra and Ben hold her ring up to the light.

FEMALE CHORUS: High up on a steel crane, the billboard workers finish up for the night.

MALE CHORUS: The workers do not look down this time, as they are themselves dumbfounded by the stunning work that has emerged before their eyes.

The Chorus embodies the scene in the billboard as its description progresses.

FEMALE CHORUS: In a black and white photograph a thousand feet wide, in shades of pearl- and oyster-greys, amid reams of white cotton sheets, the girl in the white slip dress and the man in the button-fly boxers lie tangled together in a dishevelled sleigh bed.

MALE CHORUS: Through leaded Dutch doors, a cloud of locusts is visible in the distance. The locusts are barely outrunning a charcoal-grey cyclone that careens over flooded city streets, toward the couple where they lie.

FEMALE CHORUS: Around each of the lovers' perfect pale necks, a shiny ball hangs from a delicate chain.

MALE CHORUS: Below the photo, a discreet caption reads:

CHORUS: *(pointed pause, then super-commercial)* For the pain.

MALE CHORUS: The young newlywed husband turns his wife's tear-streaked face up toward the beautiful billboard.

MALE CHORUS (AS NEWLYWED MAN): Look up there. What do you see?

She sees the billboard.

FEMALE CHORUS (AS NEWLYWED WOMAN): Oooooh! I want one!

ALL: (*singing*)
Touch me, baby ...

FEMALE CHORUS: That night, a strange new current of air blows across the earth's surface, and deep in the earth's core, a river of molten lava is chilled and turns to stone.

ALL: (*singing*)
Touch me, baby ...
Touch me, baby ...
Touch me, baby ...

Music out. Lights fade to black, very briefly.

Jewels

Lights snap to a chilly bright. The Chorus darts swiftly to stage left and right. Cassandra is draped across the foot of the bed. Ben holds Cassandra's hair back.

CASSANDRA: I'm so sorry.

BEN: Don't be sorry.

CASSANDRA: I couldn't get up from the bed.

BEN: Don't be sorry.

CASSANDRA: (*turning to him*) I've never felt so ill.

BEN: Look at your eyes.

CASSANDRA: What do you see?

BEN: They're sparkling.

CASSANDRA: I'm a monster.

BEN: A beautiful monster.

CASSANDRA: I'm vile.

BEN: These drops that fell from your lips –

CASSANDRA: Poison.

BEN: Jewels. It's as though a stream of jewels fell from your lips.

CASSANDRA: I'm a monster.

BEN: You're only being human.

CASSANDRA: What kind of human?

MALE CHORUS: Ben gazes into the basin. It is filled with beautiful jewels.

BEN: A beautiful human. (*turning back to her*) Look at your eyes!

CASSANDRA: They must be bright with fever.

BEN: What?

CASSANDRA: My eyes see both ways.

BEN: What?

CASSANDRA: Don't worry, I'm sturdy that way.

BEN: What?

CASSANDRA: Lie down on me. I fear I'll fly away.

FEMALE CHORUS: The next morning, Cassandra calls in sick.

When a Rabbit Dies

MALE CHORUS: That night, Ben comes home from work to find Cassandra rocking a dying rabbit in her arms.

Ben enters. He halts.

CASSANDRA: (*not looking at Ben*) I didn't have a fever. And I didn't have a rash. And yet ...

BEN: (*hoarsely*) Yes?

CASSANDRA: I feared that there was some strange bug in me. Some strange creature living in the water in my flesh. Swimming in my veins. Creeping toward my brain.

BEN: (*paralyzed*) Yes?

She lifts the dying rabbit and rocks it in her arms.

CASSANDRA: It's difficult to tell them apart sometimes, these sicknesses, these creatures. So I went and got this rabbit here. And now, of course, I'm sure. This new creature in me ...

She tears up. She looks at Ben.

CASSANDRA: It is a human creature.

Music in: 'When a Rabbit Dies.' Nursery-rhyme sweet. Ben moves gingerly toward Cassandra, clearly overcome. He sings.

BEN: (*gently*)

When a rabbit dies, all the world stops spinning.
In your round little belly, there's a new life swimming.
There's a new moon shining on your thickening thighs,
There's a new love growing when a rabbit dies.

CHORUS:

Uh uh oh,
Uh uh oh (*continues under*)

CASSANDRA: (*sniffling*)

When a rabbit dies, it's a perfect test for
When a girl suspects she's in her first trimester.
There's a bunny poison in her dark fecund womb,
Life's elixir lightly reaping rabbit doom.

CHORUS:

Doom doom doom.

MALE CHORUS:

Doo bee doo bee.

CHORUS:

Doom doom doom.

CASSANDRA:

When a bunny dies, a girl can't help but
Feel a little sad for the convulsing rabbit.

BEN:

For a bunny's terror as its life slips away,

BEN AND CASSANDRA: *(big smiles)*

But a rabbit's ruin marks our brightest day!

MALE CHORUS: Ben and Cassandra race out into the street, where they begin shopping madly. Salespeople, ice cream vendors and all the citizens in the street share in the delight and rapture only an impending baby can evoke!

ALL: *(singing)*

When a rabbit dies, there's a new life growing,

FEMALE CHORUS (AS MATERNITY SHOP GIRL):

Means some nice new dresses,

CASSANDRA:

'Cuz I'll soon be showing!

BEN:

Means some nice massages,

MALE CHORUS (AS ICE CREAM VENDOR):

And ten types of ice cream,

ALL:

When a rabbit squeals its final silent scream!
When a rabbit dies, when a bunny's poisoned,

FEMALE CHORUS (AS TOY SHOP GIRL):

Means you'll have to buy a thousand plastic toys and

MALE CHORUS (AS GARBAGE MAN):

Means a pile of diapers seventeen storeys high!

ALL:

Means a new life living when a rabbit dies!

ALL:

When a rabbit dies, all the world stops spinning.
In her round little belly there's a new life swimming.
There's a new moon shining on her thickening thighs,
There's a new love growing when a rabbit …

CASSANDRA AND BEN:

Di-i-i-ies.

CHORUS:

Doom doom doom.

MALE CHORUS:

Doo bee doo bee.

CHORUS:

Doom doom doom.

CASSANDRA AND BEN:

Uh oh oh.

ALL:

Doom!

Cassandra sighs happily.
Music out. Ben and Cassandra exit.

Quicksilver Consolidated

MALE CHORUS: One trimester later.

Music in: 'Quicksilver Consolidated.' Even faster, even jinglier.

MALE CHORUS: (*to Female Chorus, in greeting*) Morning!

FEMALE CHORUS: (*to Male Chorus*) Morning!

BOTH: (*to the audience*) Morning.

FEMALE CHORUS: High above the city streets, through the vaulted hallways of the tallest office tower, atop the highest cottony clouds and almost up inside the heavens themselves –

MALE CHORUS: – the employees of Quicksilver Consolidated fly about in that early morning kind of way. Their hearts soar and their smooth cheeks flush with dense particles of oxygen that float on currents of purified, vaporized, ionized air.

MALE CHORUS (AS EMPLOYEE 1): Good morning, Quicksilver Consolidated –

FEMALE CHORUS (AS EMPLOYEE 2): Good morning, Quicksilver Consolidated!

MALE CHORUS: The complex choreography of the workers has been rendered even more complicated by the addition of a dozen new interns: young as saplings, smart as whips.

MALE CHORUS (AS INTERN 1): I'll make the joe, you file those!

FEMALE CHORUS (AS INTERN 2): All right, I'll file these!

CHORUS (AS INTERNS): (*singing*)

Thick sweet-scented candles light the
Labyrinth from desolation.
Speedy little scooters ease a
Creeping sense of suffocation!

MALE CHORUS (AS INTERN 1): I'm sorry, sir, but Mr. Cordair hasn't yet returned from his honeymoon.

FEMALE CHORUS (AS INTERN 2): Though we do expect him back real soon.

MALE CHORUS (AS INTERN 1): I certainly will.

FEMALE CHORUS (AS INTERN 2): I certainly will.

BOTH (AS INTERNS): You have a nice day, too!

Music out.

MALE CHORUS: A flock of interns huddles by the water cooler.

Hushed, swiftly.

MALE CHORUS (AS INTERN 3): I heard he married a salesgirl from The Abyss.

FEMALE CHORUS (AS INTERN 4): Ben married a salesgirl?

MALE CHORUS (AS INTERN 5): Hey, don't knock it! They say since he met her the music of the spheres has been spilling from his lips!

FEMALE CHORUS (AS INTERN 6): And Quicksilver's last quarter was killer!

MALE CHORUS (AS JUSTIN): Well geez, I'd date a girl from The Abyss if it meant the music of the spheres would start spilling from *my* lips!

FEMALE CHORUS (AS EPIPHANY): I'd get a *job* at The Abyss if it meant I could kiss a pair of sphere-spilling lips like his!

Ben enters. All gasp.

BEN: Morning, Justin.

JUSTIN: Morning, Ben.

BEN: Morning, Epiphany.

EPIPHANY: Morning, Ben. Did you have a nice honeymoon, Ben?

BEN: I had a glorious week, a glorious week of the most outrageous joy. Why, I might just be the happiest man in the world right now!

EPIPHANY: (*whispering to Justin*) I hear she's pregnant!

JUSTIN: Piff! How rude!

MALE CHORUS: (*embodying Skeet, covertly*) Over by the latte machine, Skeet and Charlize sip steaming Ethiopians and gossip about Ben's meteoric rise through the Quicksilver ranks over the past few months.

FEMALE CHORUS: (*embodying Charlize*) They eye him with that particular blend of envy and respect that is inspired by those who are undeniably touched by genius.

MALE CHORUS: Ben is greeted by his sassy new assistants –

FEMALE CHORUS (AS SASSY ASSISTANT 1): Spring water, Mr. Cordair?

MALE CHORUS (AS SASSY ASSISTANT 2): Some ylang-ylang?

FEMALE CHORUS: – who sweep Ben into his brand-new corner office –

MALE CHORUS: (*almost erotically*) – which is exhilaratingly perched on design's cutting edge.

FEMALE CHORUS: They open their laptops and wait.

Over the following, the Chorus types each word Ben says into laptops.

BEN: (*swiftly*) In the space between the products lies, I believe, a truth about humanity. And we, my bright young friends, are uncovering the anagrams of human desire. We are untangling their intricate webs. We have channelled our energies into the universe and the universe is offering itself up to us. And I am filled with wonder. I am filled with awe.

FEMALE CHORUS: Ben gazes through the window and watches a solo cloud tumble above the rest and transform itself into the shape of a baby, indicating that the fruit of Ben's perfect loins is on his dazzled mind.

Music in: 'The Abyss' reprise.

MALE CHORUS: And at six o'clock sharp, Ben collects his pretty wife from The Abyss.

BEN AND CHORUS: (*singing*)

In nothingness lies everything …

Sunday in Semi-Residentia

Music transition: 'In Semi-Residentia.' Like 'Quicksilver,' but softer, slower and more complacent. The Chorus sings in rounds and overlapping verses, as indicated by slashes.

CHORUS:

Glowing clocks can / ohhh …
Silver pen sets / sl-o-o-ow …
Racing minds …
With memorie-e-e-e-s.

MALE CHORUS: Ben and Cassandra wander through the narrow streets of Semi-Residentia. Young families stroll through the February dusk in light summer clothing.

MALE CHORUS (AS YOUNG DAD): Nice night.

BEN AND CASSANDRA: Beautiful.

CHORUS:

Gleaming silver / o-h-h-h
Slows the speed of / ah-h-h …
Deadened eyes / in
Sets of thre-e-e-e.

'In Semi-Residentia' continues and underscores the rest of the scene.

CASSANDRA: What if it's a boy?

BEN: Then I think we should name it Michael. Or David.

CASSANDRA: Oh, I think Michael's sweet. And if it's a girl I think Margot. Or Mary.

BEN: What about Epiphany?

CASSANDRA: Epi – ? Oh … (*giggle*) I don't think I could even say that!

They stop. He points.

BEN: That's it. That's the house where I was born.

CASSANDRA: Oh! It's sweet.

MALE CHORUS: A young couple wanders by with a very tiny baby in a stroller. (*Cassandra watches the stroller.*) They carry tins of Varathane for their new cedar deck and vinyl trim for their new sliding door.

BEN: (*still pointing*) It used to be bigger but they split it in two.

CASSANDRA: So that two families could live there!

BEN: Yes. But one of the families sold their half.

CASSANDRA: Hence the café.

FEMALE CHORUS: A young couple emerges from the café with steaming lattes and a very tiny baby in a harness.

CASSANDRA: It's very beautiful. Inside. The café. It looks cozy.

BEN: They built this café, and then they bought halves of houses on every city block. From cash-strapped families whose reaches exceeded their grasps. And they built these cafés on the foundations of shattered dreams.

CASSANDRA: Oh …

BEN: Yes. (*a little sad*) It's what gives the coffee its bite, they say.

MALE CHORUS: A young family passes. A mother, a father and two cross-eyed little boys. The boys push dolls in tiny strollers that have been given to them so that they will be more nurturing.

BEN: That video store used to be a grocery. The man who ran it used to give my brother and me free bananas.

CASSANDRA: (*wistfully*) Yes, I remember bananas.

Ben gazes at the video store. Cassandra watches the Female Chorus, who strolls by with a baby.

MALE CHORUS: A new mother sways sensually down the street, high on pheromones and endorphins. She wears a see-through dress that reveals a little white slip beneath. In her arms she carries a very tiny baby. The baby wears gossamer sleepers that reveal the little white diaper beneath. The baby isn't even conscious of it.

BEN: This used to be the edge of town. We used to go away every weekend. To the cottage.

CASSANDRA: Cot-tage?

BEN: But then the country got farther away. When the neighbourhood became very popular, what with all the video stores and cafés, more and more families moved to this edge of town and built their houses, and soon it took a whole day to get to the country. And then two days. And then four. And finally my parents were forced to sell the cottage. And where it once was, there is now …

CASSANDRA: … a café?

BEN: (*admiringly*) So clever.

MALE CHORUS: In a nearby Astroturfed yard, the cross-eyed boys have been sent outside to play with their dolls. The boys stand at opposite ends of the yard and race toward each other as fast as they can, until the tiny strollers collide and the dolls go flying: one sails through the neighbours' brand-new sliding glass door, the other stuns a three-legged squirrel senseless.

CASSANDRA: You're sad.

BEN: I'm moved. It's all so beautiful now. I think it's beautiful. All the families, in all their homes ... and so many more of them than when I lived here.

CASSANDRA: Their tiny, cozy homes.

BEN: When we left, I swore I'd come back here someday. To live.

CASSANDRA: (*softly*) I never dreamed that I'd wind up here.

FEMALE CHORUS: The distinctive scent of Varathane wafts in the air.

BEN: It's a beautiful world, sometimes. The way things go.

CASSANDRA: Yes. (*looking at Ben*) Lucky me ...

FEMALE CHORUS: Something does a somersault inside Cassandra's belly.

Cassandra grips Ben's arm.

CASSANDRA: Oh!

BEN: What's the matter?

CASSANDRA: Nothing. It's nothing. I just feel a bit funny.

BEN: Morning sickness?

CASSANDRA: Love sickness. (*She lies, sweetly.*)

FEMALE CHORUS: Ben holds Cassandra protectively in his arms. They stare into each other's eyes.

MALE CHORUS: And so they do not notice as a motorist, trapped for five years in the labyrinth of one-way streets, lurches from his car and collapses in front of the café, twitching, dehydrated and fatally lonely.

BEN: Would you like to have a steamed milk?

CASSANDRA: Yes! Please! It looks so cozy in there!

FEMALE CHORUS: Ben holds the door open for a family leaving the café with paper cups filled with steaming soy drinks and little paper bags filled with cookies made with rainforest nuts. A happy mother, a happy father, two pigtailed twins and a tiny eight-limbed toddler in a stroller.

Music swells.

ALL:

Little tiny telephones send
Words of love through time and spa-a-a-a-ace.

MALE CHORUS (AS FATHER): (*to eight-limbed toddler*) No, punkin, we can't go to the amusement park tonight.

FEMALE CHORUS (AS MOTHER): It's going to snow!

CASSANDRA: (*softly*) Oh!

ALL:

Minivans and four-wheel drive make
Baby's world a safer pla-a-a-a-ace.

CASSANDRA: (*softly*) Look at the sky!

ALL:

Ah ohh!

Music out.

MALE CHORUS: Two weeks later. In their new home in Semi-Residentia.

FEMALE CHORUS: Ben is in bed with an unopened gardening book in his lap.

MALE CHORUS: Cassandra sits by a window, drying her hair with a downy cotton towel.

FEMALE CHORUS: She gazes through the window and watches the glowing aphids dance about the branches of the semi-residential trees.

BEN: If you had to pick one, what would you rather do: live a long time moderately happy, or live a shorter time wildly happy?

CASSANDRA: Um … I'd rather live a shorter time wildly happy!

BEN: Me too.

They smile at each other. Ben returns to his book, Cassandra to her aphids. Pause.

BEN: If you had to pick one, what would you rather be: beautiful forever but senile at sixty, or ugly at forty but piercingly intelligent forever?

CASSANDRA: Oooh … That's too hard! *(little pause)* I have one!

BEN: Shoot.

CASSANDRA: Which would you rather experience: true beauty, or debilitating regret?

BEN: (*baffled, not by the question, but by the fact that she asked it*) Well ... that's easy.

CASSANDRA: Oh, of course! I got it wrong! You do another one.

BEN: Okay. If you had to pick one, which would you rather be: lonely or frightened?

CASSANDRA: You mean ... half-alive or horribly alive?

BEN: Well ... sure.

CASSANDRA: I'd rather be horribly alive!

BEN: Me too.

They smile at each other. Little pause.

CASSANDRA: Ah! All right! I have one!

BEN: Shoot.

CASSANDRA: Which would you rather be responsible for: the salvation of the planet ... or its destruction?

BEN: (*little pause*) Well ...

CASSANDRA: Did I get it wrong again?

BEN: Well ...

CASSANDRA: (*sighs*) You do another!

BEN: If you had to pick one, which would you rather be: alone or irritated?

CASSANDRA: You mean alone or ... (*dryly*) with a companion?

BEN: Well …

CASSANDRA: Ah! If you had to pick one, what would you rather do: die young and leave a beautiful corpse, or die young and leave a ravaged corpse!

BEN: I …

CASSANDRA: Ahh! I got it wrong *again*!

BEN: There, there. It's just a game.

CASSANDRA: (*frustrated*) What am I doing wrong?

BEN: The questions you ask have answers that are too easy to … (*gently*) The answers are implicit. Explicit. There's no game to them.

CASSANDRA: As opposed to your questions?

BEN: Which are puzzling. Challenging. They're six-of-one, half-a-dozen-of-the-other questions. They present two realities that are not necessarily opposing, but are mutually exclusive.

Pause.

CASSANDRA: Well then they're cruel.

Pause.

BEN: Why cruel?

CASSANDRA: Because you say, If you had to pick one. As though there were a choice.

Ben is baffled.

CASSANDRA: We live but once in this world. In each case, we must live one and only one of those mutually exclusive realities. Half-alive *or* horribly alive. Lonely *or* irritated. You can't have neither. You can't have both. You must have one or the other. There's *no* other way!

Pause.

Is there?

Pause.

BEN: You're angry.

CASSANDRA: (*chilly*) No I'm not.

BEN: Then why are your hands like that?

CASSANDRA: Like what?

BEN: In fists. You're angry.

CASSANDRA: I said I'm not.

BEN: Then why are you crying?

CASSANDRA: (*peevishly*) Because I don't want to fight.

BEN: Why don't you want to fight?

CASSANDRA: Because. I don't want to die alone.

MALE CHORUS: Cassandra drifts through the faux-Dutch sliding doors and out onto the pine vérité deck. She gazes out over the green backyards, the shining Land Rovers in the driveways, the little strollers nestled on their porches and the 1,000 sleeping golden retrievers whose 3,999 paws twitch, and in whose dreams dance visions of cornered, clawless cats.

Ben crosses to her.

BEN: What's the matter?

CASSANDRA: Nothing. It's nothing. I'm tired is all; I've got lots on my mind. Baby swim … Gymboree …

BEN: A girl's got a right to a little distraction.

CASSANDRA: A girl's got a right to cold feet when she's pregnant.

BEN: Cold as she wants.

CASSANDRA: (*hushed*) Two blocks of ice.

MALE CHORUS: A barely perceptible earthquake sends gentle tremors shuddering through the sleepy neighbourhood. Ben wraps his arms around Cassandra. The tremors subside.

CASSANDRA: (*touching the flesh of his cheek*) Forgive me.

They go inside and move to the bed.

FEMALE CHORUS: He does.

Delicate Chain

MALE CHORUS: One week later. In The Abyss. Cassandra floats through pools of halogen light.

FEMALE CHORUS: A cunning ensemble camouflages the gentle swelling in Cassandra's belly –

Cassandra holds en pointe fixe *for a moment, revealing little or no indication of any swelling at all.*

MALE CHORUS: – and a magical elixir of hormones and pheromones flows through her veins, rendering her the perfect model of harmony and calm.

FEMALE CHORUS: A heavy package arrives by special courier.

MALE CHORUS (AS COURIER): Morning, Cassandra.

CASSANDRA: Morning, Tom.

MALE CHORUS (AS TOM): Nice day out.

CASSANDRA: Beautiful.

FEMALE CHORUS: And as Cassandra signs for the package –

MALE CHORUS (AS TOM): (*observing*) – the phone rings.

CASSANDRA: Hello?

BEN: Hello.

Cassandra giggles.

How are you?

Cassandra giggles again.

Is everything all right?

CASSANDRA: No. Really. I'm fine.

BEN: Shall I take you out for dinner tonight?

CASSANDRA: Oooh, yes, please!

BEN: Six o'clock?

CASSANDRA: Sharp.

BEN: Happy, darling?

CASSANDRA: Delirious. Happy, darling?

BEN: Out of my mind.

They hang up.

FEMALE CHORUS: Cassandra eyes the package that Tom has left behind.

MALE CHORUS: She cuts the dove-grey string that binds it.

FEMALE CHORUS: She tears the slate-grey paper that wraps it.

MALE CHORUS: Inside the package are dozens of little pearl-grey jewel boxes.

FEMALE CHORUS: Inside each jewel box, on an oyster-grey cushion, there lies a delicate chain.

MALE CHORUS: And attached to each chain, there is a gleaming –

CHORUS: – shiny ball.

Over the following, Cassandra remains perfectly still, staring at the lockets before her. She may hold one in her hands. The Chorus flanks her.

FEMALE CHORUS (AS FEMALE PATRON): (*staring at display*) I heard they started in the clubs. I heard they went into the clubs to see what the kids were wearing. What they liked. I heard they were first worn by artists.

MALE CHORUS (AS MALE PATRON): Ar-tists?

FEMALE PATRON: Yes, artists. Sculptors? Painters? Poets? (*beat*) Those who once engaged in writing a detailed history of the future because of their acute perceptions of the nature of the present? (*sigh*) Because of their age-old ability to sidestep the violence of progress with full awareness?

MALE PATRON: Oh, artists!

FEMALE PATRON: Yes, artists!

MALE PATRON: Yes, I remember artists! They had those, um ...

FEMALE PATRON: Stormy temperaments?

MALE PATRON: No. I mean those ... those ...

FEMALE PATRON: Gouging debts?

MALE PATRON: No, I mean those ... those fanciful preferences!

FEMALE PATRON: Oh, yes. The fanciful preferences. Yes, those were sweet. I believe there's one in the window right now.

MALE PATRON: An artist?

FEMALE PATRON: No, silly. A photograph of an artist.

She takes him downstage.

They hired them to model the clothing. And the artists used the money they received for posing to buy ointments, which salved the wounds that had been created by their hands clawing at their own faces. Or to buy smart caps for their skulls, made cold and bare by the tearing out of their own hair. Or to pay for the medicines they took to anaesthetize the pain that emanated from the chasmic wounds in their bellies that opened up and bled endlessly due to the years and years of bitterness and bile that went before this time now, this time now when all the world shows its gratitude.

MALE PATRON: (*in disbelief*) For their art?

FEMALE PATRON: Don't be silly. For the aesthetic contributions these 'originals' made to what have come to be known as 'the classics.'

MALE PATRON: The classics?

FEMALE PATRON: Yes, the classics. Blue jeans? Chinos? The little black dress?

MALE PATRON: Oh, the classics! (*He reads.*) Sylvia: Poet. In Abyss denim, ribbed turtleneck and ... (*over-pronouncing*) Sphere Pendant.

FEMALE PATRON: (*whispering*) I heard they filled these little lockets with drops of fatal poison – hemlock, mercury, arsenic – and laced the lethal potions with morphine.

MALE PATRON: Morphine?

FEMALE PATRON: (*she almost hisses*) For the pain.

MALE PATRON: Mmmm.

FEMALE PATRON: I want one!

Lights shift radically. Cassandra is suddenly isolated in a single pool of halogen light. The Chorus crosses to Ben, who is cast in a cold November diffusion.

MALE CHORUS: Meanwhile, ten blocks away and a thousand storeys above, a swarm of hummingbirds hovers outside Ben's office and flirts with their reflections.

FEMALE CHORUS: The speakerphone chirps.

MALE CHORUS: The call is from another more glimmering city where, in an even more heavenly office in a taller office tower that well nigh scrapes the dove-grey sky, the board of Quicksilver Consortium has gathered to –

The board's voices are amplified, echoing.

FEMALE CHORUS (AS BOARD MEMBER 1): – congratulate Ben.

Little pause.

BEN: (*softly*) Thank you.

MALE CHORUS: (*softly*) They murmur praise for Ben's work. They say it is –

FEMALE CHORUS (AS BOARD MEMBER 1): (*softly*) – almost like poetry.

MALE CHORUS (AS BOARD MEMBER 2): Almost like poetry.

FEMALE CHORUS: (AS BOARD MEMBER 1): Almost like art.

BEN: (*uncertain*) Thank you.

FEMALE CHORUS: Ten blocks away and a thousand storeys below, Cassandra lifts a gleaming shiny ball from its pearl-grey box. She dangles it from its delicate chain.

Cassandra stares at the dangling pendant.

MALE CHORUS: It spins and spins until its chain unravels, then spins the other way.

Music in: 'Snow Song' reprise. Discordant, spooky.

CHORUS: (*singing*)
Uh uh, oh, uh uh …

Widow in a Tank Top

The Chorus continues to sing 'uh oh's through the scene. Cassandra laces a freestyle melody through the narration, in perfect disharmony with the Chorus.

CASSANDRA:
La, la la, la la la la …

FEMALE CHORUS: Later that day, Cassandra leaves work early.

MALE CHORUS: Three hours.

FEMALE CHORUS: A thick fog rolls along the sidewalks and swirls in the sparkling streets. Cassandra drifts along, very, very, very slowly.

MALE CHORUS: A sudden gust of wind hurtles through the streets and sends the fog twisting skyward. Way, way in the distance, the graveyard appears in Cassandra's mind's eye. She stops and thinks *(little pause)* and keeps walking along.

FEMALE CHORUS: Then she thinks again.

Cassandra moves back toward the graveyard position she first held in 'Snow Song.'

MALE CHORUS: And as the fog descends once more, Cassandra drifts toward the graveyard gates.

CASSANDRA: (*sotto voce, singing*)

Seems the sky keeps falling down ...

She kneels. The lights dim and the music swells. She whispers things to the grave that the audience cannot hear. She caresses the earth as though it were alive. The song finishes and the music stops. Cassandra notices the music has stopped. She looks at the Chorus, and at Ben. In uncomfortable silence, Ben takes a seat centre stage.

Flounder

MALE CHORUS: That night, Cassandra is late for dinner.

Cassandra takes a seat beside Ben.

BEN: Three hours.

FEMALE CHORUS: Cassandra apologizes for being late and kisses Ben on the cheek.

She does.

MALE CHORUS: Absently.

Cassandra looks at the Male Chorus.

FEMALE CHORUS: Cassandra explains about all the appointments she had that afternoon, and about the prenatal classes she has been looking into, which are the reasons why she was so late.

Ben and Cassandra look at the Female Chorus.

MALE CHORUS: (*very close to Ben*) Ben tries to hold Cassandra's hand across the table.

BEN: Dirt falls from under Cassandra's pink, polished nails.

FEMALE CHORUS: Cassandra says the dirt is a special nail treatment from New Zealand and lies about how she spontaneously got a manicure, which is also why she was so late, and that even though she *told* them at the salon that she had a dinner date, the manicurists said the dirt pack had to set!

Cassandra and Ben look at the Female Chorus.

FEMALE CHORUS: (*embodying teenage girl*) A covert of teenage girls wander past the window.

MALE CHORUS: Cassandra cannot take her eyes off the shiny balls hanging from their slender necks.

Ben nuzzles Cassandra's ear. The Male Chorus moves in very close to them.

MALE CHORUS: (*softly*) And so she does not hear the love words that her husband whispers into her seashell-pink ears.

Cassandra looks right at the Male Chorus, who is very close to her. The Female Chorus approaches the table with menus.

FEMALE CHORUS: (*embodying waitress*) The waitress informs them that the restaurant is out of cod and sole.

MALE CHORUS: (*embodying maitre d'*) The maitre d' suggests the flounder.

FEMALE CHORUS: A starving man wanders in from the street.

MALE CHORUS: (*embodying starving man*) He drinks the liquid wax from a candle, then complains to the maitre d' that:

MALE CHORUS (AS STARVING MAN): THERE ARE TOO MANY PEOPLE IN THE WOR-R-R-RLD!

Music in: a horrible, atonal version of 'The Shiny Ball Song.'

FEMALE CHORUS: The band plays, and Cassandra begs:

CASSANDRA: Dance with me.

FEMALE CHORUS: (*softly, very close to Ben*) And as they rise, Ben sees the dirt fall from his pretty wife's knees –

Ben escorts Cassandra to the dance floor.

MALE CHORUS: – and notices the sun on her cheeks –

FEMALE CHORUS: – and he asks Cassandra if she still loves him.

Ben takes her in his arms.

MALE CHORUS: Cassandra asks:

CASSANDRA: What *kind* of love?

Ben and Cassandra dance to the 'The Shiny Ball Song' aberration.

FEMALE CHORUS: Meanwhile, back in the graveyard, as twilight falls and night chills the air, the warmth from Cassandra's body finally leaves the earth where she had knelt, and Cassandra's dead love rolls over in his dusty bed –

MALE CHORUS: (*softly, cutting in and touching Cassandra*) – and nothing will ever be the same.

Cassandra moans in pain. She falls to floor and stares at the Male Chorus. Ben scoops her up.
Snap to:

Have You Been in Anything?

In a car, in interior light, Cassandra writhes, her head in Ben's lap.

MALE CHORUS: (*embodying taxi driver*) In a taxi. On a cellphone.

BEN: (*into the phone, in a controlled panic*) We need a doctor.

FEMALE CHORUS (AS EMERGENCY OPERATOR): (*insouciant*) Have you been in anything?

BEN: I beg your pardon?

EMERGENCY OPERATOR: Have you been in anything a doctor might have seen? A movie, a television show, a political campaign, a major sports event, a trial?

BEN: No.

EMERGENCY OPERATOR: I'm sorry, the doctors are very busy and mustn't be bothered. You could try emergency.

Pause.

BEN: (*emphatically*) I have a lot of money.

Pause.

EMERGENCY OPERATOR: Could you hold, please?

MALE CHORUS: In a hospital corridor. Ben and Cassandra have skipped the lineup to emergency because of all the money Ben has.

CASSANDRA: (*writhing*) Lucky me …

MALE CHORUS: And well-connected cardiac patients, well-heeled reconstructive patients and high-priority mental patients share in the delight and rapture only an impending baby can evoke!

FEMALE CHORUS: The nurses have attached an ultrasound to Cassandra. They move it all over her round little belly, looking for the baby. They cannot find it.

BEN: What's the matter?

MALE CHORUS (AS MALE NURSE): Pressure is falling.

BEN: Something's the matter.

FEMALE CHORUS (AS FEMALE NURSE): Heart rate is falling.

CASSANDRA: Oh, dear. The stars are all falling.

BEN: What do you want? What do you *need*?

CASSANDRA: I want to look out my window and see a pie, a dog, a field, a horse.

BEN: Get her a doctor.

MALE NURSE: Her body is chaos.

BEN: Get her a doctor.

NURSES: There's none to be found.

BEN: She's dying, isn't she?

MALE NURSE: Compared to whom?

CASSANDRA: Hold me down, I'm flying away!

Music in: 'Cry, Cry, Cry,' a variation on 'Consummation,' but quicker and more urgent.

CHORUS:

Feel the wild thing in the blackness,
Feel it wriggle, feel it writhe.
Feel its neck, which when it moves,
Grows tangled in the ties that bind.

CASSANDRA: (*grabbing the Male Chorus's arm*) Where is my husband?

BEN: (*bellowing*) Where are the doctors?

MALE NURSE: She's losing ground.

CASSANDRA: Oh, the earth!

MALE NURSE: She's falling fast!

CASSANDRA: I'm flying away!

BEN: Look in my eyes. What do you see?

Cassandra looks into Ben's eyes and gasps.

CASSANDRA: Sparkles!

She faints.

CHORUS:

Feel it thrash its purple legs and
Purple arms, they're built to swim.
Feel it wrestle, feel it panic,
Baby needs some oxygen.

CHORUS AND BEN:

Come on, baby,
Come on, honey,
Come on down into the light.
Smell how sweet and strange the air is,
Take a breath and cry cry cry.

Cassandra screams an agonized, desperate variation on the Kama Sutra warble from 'Consummation.' Music out. Pause.

FEMALE CHORUS: The baby is born. It is tiny. (*She looks into her cupped hands, where she's palmed the light source.*) About an inch and a half long.

All look into the Female Chorus's hands.

FEMALE CHORUS: And it glows.

The nurses and Ben gaze at the glowing baby. Cassandra leaves her body and wanders through the room. As the scene goes on, when the nurses and Ben speak to Cassandra, they speak to where she should be as opposed to where she is.

Music in: 'Smaller and Stranger.' Delicate, like a baby-powder commercial.

NURSES: (*singing softly*)

Smaller and stranger is she,
Smaller and stranger than we.
But in her tiny little frame,
Life's juice is flowing just the same.

NURSES:

Smaller and stranger is she,
Smaller and stranger than we.

BEN: She's perfect.

FEMALE NURSE: She's beautiful.

MALE NURSE: (*to Cassandra*) Just like her mom.

FEMALE NURSE: Yes. Only littler.

Over the following verse, Cassandra peers over the others' shoulders at the baby in the Female Chorus's hands.

CHORUS AND BEN:

Stranger than magic is this
Marvellous wee little miss.
Tiny vessels barely there,
Her ventricles are angel hairs.

BEN: Look at her perfect little fingers.

MALE NURSE: And her perfect toes.

FEMALE NURSE: All twenty of them.

BEN: Twenty toes?

FEMALE NURSES: No, no! Twenty digits!

Cassandra wanders as far away as possible.

CHORUS AND BEN:

Out of the darkness she's flung.
How does the air find her lungs?

Must be something in the breeze
That makes this creature yearn to breathe.

FEMALE NURSE: Look at how she grips your finger with her strong little arms!

MALE NURSE: Just wrapped around your little finger!

BEN: And her eyes!

MALE NURSE: Her eyes!

FEMALE NURSE: Her eyes! Just like her dad's!

MALE NURSE: But the colour of mom's!

BEN: I could fall into her eyes!

FEMALE NURSE: Her eyes are bigger than her stomach!

CHORUS AND BEN:

Smaller and stranger is she,
Smaller and stranger than we.

CASSANDRA:

But look at how her little hands
Make fists I somehow understand.

BEN: Oh no.

FEMALE NURSE: What's wrong?

BEN: I think she's crying.

MALE NURSE: Those are little tears!

FEMALE NURSE: Yes, they're tears!

Cassandra dawdles reluctantly back toward the bed.

BEN: What's she doing with her mouth?

MALE NURSE: She's just trying to wail.

BEN: Why can't she wail?

FEMALE NURSE: She's too tiny! (*baby-talk to baby*) Her vocal cords haven't developed yet!

BEN: So she'll wail?

FEMALE NURSE: Oh, she'll wail! Don't you worry!

BEN: Why is she trying to wail?

FEMALE NURSE: Same reason anybody wails. (*She gives the glowing baby to Cassandra.*) Because she's hungry.

ALL:

Heart small as a grain of sand
Pumps blood through her transparent hands.
Watch her shining in the night,
Like a beacon in the blight.
Smaller and stranger by far,
Stranger than secrets you are.

CASSANDRA:

But don't you know, my little friend,
This pain you feel will
Never end?

MALE NURSE: She's perfect.

FEMALE NURSE: She's perfect.

BEN AND CASSANDRA: She's exactly like us.

FEMALE CHORUS: Ben and Cassandra are given the baby to take home because there is no more room in the incubators.

MALE CHORUS: No matter how much money you have.

Lights fade slowly as the baby's bassinet is presented. Lights go to black, save for the glowing baby in Cassandra's hands. Cassandra places the baby in the bassinet. Cassandra sits down on a chair that has been placed beside the bassinet. She is cast in the baby's glow. Ben stands in his Quicksilver position, upstage left. He is barely lit. The Chorus sits on the lip of the stage, also barely visible. Their manner shifts at this point: they become more direct, more serious, as though they are telling a story they wish they didn't have to tell. All performers speak directly to the audience.

Bringing up Baby

FEMALE CHORUS: Although she tries, Cassandra has no real feelings for the tiny creature that is her child.

BEN: Though she tries.

MALE CHORUS: She doesn't hold the child much.

FEMALE CHORUS: It makes the baby cry.

CASSANDRA: It just feels awkward.

FEMALE CHORUS: And though she feeds it –

BEN: – whenever it cries –

MALE CHORUS: – with minute bottles of formula –

CASSANDRA: (*to the audience, parenthetically maternal*) She's too tiny to breast-feed.

CHORUS AND BEN: – the baby fails to thrive.

They all sit for the briefest of moments in the glow of the tiny child. They do not look at her.

CASSANDRA: Yes, yes it does.

FEMALE CHORUS: Soon after the child is born, Ben goes back to work.

MALE CHORUS: But not before he asks Cassandra:

BEN: Are you sure you'll be all right?

FEMALE CHORUS: And not before she replies:

CASSANDRA: (*brightly*) No. Really. I don't feel a thing.

FEMALE CHORUS: For some-odd mornings, Cassandra strolls her weeping child to café patios, where they sit in the shadows of trees. She rocks the baby's stroller back and forth –

MALE CHORUS: – and studies the motions of the other young mothers sitting with babies in strollers in the shadows of trees.

FEMALE CHORUS: For some-odd afternoons, Cassandra sits in the baby's nursery.

CASSANDRA: By the window.

BEN: Through which the graveyard is visible.

CASSANDRA: But only off in the distance.

FEMALE CHORUS: And only in her mind's eye.

MALE CHORUS: Cassandra rocks the baby's bassinet.

FEMALE CHORUS: A persistent breeze blows through the nursery window.

MALE CHORUS: The muslin curtains tickle at the vinyl trim.

Cassandra rises.

FEMALE CHORUS: For some-odd twilights, Cassandra wanders out onto the pine vérité deck and gazes up into the lime-green sky.

BEN: Where her marvellous eyes see visions.

From this point on, movement and staging may creep back in very gradually. Cassandra and Ben particularly will embody the descriptions of the action.

MALE CHORUS: For some-odd nights, Ben comes home from work bearing tropical flowers for his pretty wife –

CASSANDRA: Bluebells!

MALE CHORUS: – and fuzzy, squeaky toys for his baby girl.

FEMALE CHORUS: Ducks.

MALE CHORUS: Lambs.

FEMALE CHORUS: Bears.

CASSANDRA: Zebras.

BEN: Their eyes glow in the dark.

Ben makes an unnatural squeaky animal noise as he places a bear into the bassinet.

MALE CHORUS: Ben brings home spinning mobiles of all the planets and stars.

FEMALE CHORUS: Tiny universes.

BEN: Of which the tiny glowing baby is the centre.

CASSANDRA: The house is always clean.

FEMALE CHORUS: Cassandra's hair is always done.

CASSANDRA: The baby is always fed and dry.

BEN: But though she's always fed and dry –

CASSANDRA: (*aside*) – and so the baby will not cry –

FEMALE CHORUS: – Cassandra finds inventive ways not to touch her little girl.

CASSANDRA: (*holding her hands out helplessly*) The manicurists said the dirt pack had to set.

ALL BUT CASSANDRA: And baby fails to thrive.

Ben and the Chorus now move back to Quicksilver positions.

FEMALE CHORUS: For some-odd months, ninety-five blocks away and ten thousand storeys above, Ben is greeted by his newer, more celestial assistants, whose physical exquisiteness is matched only by their soaring IQs.

CHORUS (AS CELESTIAL ASSISTANTS): (*offering*) Glacier water?

Over the following, the Male and Female Chorus do not take their eyes from Ben. They type speedily on their laptops.

BEN: (*softly, swiftly*) If in the patterns –

MALE CHORUS (AS CELESTIAL ASSISTANT 1): – of the products?

BEN: Yes, the products. Their consumption. There lie maps, or anagrams –

FEMALE CHORUS (AS CELESTIAL ASSISTANT 2): These are unconscious?

BEN: Yes, unconscious. It is our burden, and our privilege –

CELESTIAL ASSISTANT 2: The good consumption?

BEN: Yes. It is our privilege to conjure for them –

CELESTIAL ASSISTANT 2: – make manifest for them –

BEN: – the promise of –

CELESTIAL ASSISTANT 1: The promise –

BEN: – of ... (*He clears his throat.*) We have plumbed the virtues of the skies and the trees and the seven seas.

The celestial assistants halt.

CELESTIAL ASSISTANTS: Six.

BEN: I beg your pardon?

CELESTIAL ASSISTANT 2: There were seven.

CELESTIAL ASSISTANT 1: Now there are six.

BEN: (*disconcerted*) Of course.

CELESTIAL ASSISTANT 2: (*offering, sympathetically*) Eucalyptus?

MALE CHORUS: Ben receives an emergency call.

CELESTIAL ASSISTANT 2: From home.

The Female Chorus hands Ben the phone.

BEN: Hello?

CASSANDRA: (*into phone*) I thought of a name for her: Shirley. Only I think we should spell it S-u-r-e-l-y. Give her a leg up in the world.

BEN: I don't know ...

CASSANDRA: (*genuinely*) Trust me; doubt yourself.

BEN: I beg your pardon?

CASSANDRA: I said, 'Blush free; sprout your health.' (*She hangs up.*)

The actors half-stage the following sequence.

FEMALE CHORUS: For some-odd weeks, though she manages their child and their large semi-residential house –

CASSANDRA: – and the all the errands, and cleaning, and the tradesmen who come there each and every day –

sfx: clanging knife-sharpener bell.

MALE CHORUS: RA-A-A-A-ABIT COFFINS! GET YOUR RA-A-A-A-A-ABIT COFF-F-F-FIN-NN-NS!

FEMALE CHORUS: – Ben watches his pretty wife grow pale as chalk and notes an unnatural brightness in her eyes.

MALE CHORUS: Nightly, he lies down on Cassandra and tries to keep her from flying around the room.

Ben holds Cassandra tight.

FEMALE CHORUS: Nightly, he murmurs love words into her seashell-pink ears –

Ben whispers into Cassanrda's ear.

MALE CHORUS: – while inside Cassandra's smooth white skull, death hurtles to and fro.

CASSANDRA: (*pulling her ear away from Ben's mouth, softly*) What kind of love? (*She strokes his cheek.*) Ben?

Ben and Cassandra look into each other's eyes for a moment. Cassandra slips away. For the next few scenes, Ben does not take his eyes from her.

MALE CHORUS: For some-odd weeks, Ben wakes nightly to find Cassandra somnambulating ghost-like through their beautiful *feng shuivian* home, or to hear her weeping in their emerald-green backyard, where she searches for something beneath the perfect strips of lawn.

FEMALE CHORUS: For some-odd weeks, he wakes each morning with his arms around his ice-cold wife and scrubs clumps of dirt from beneath her pretty fingernails.

CASSANDRA: (*barely audible*) Oh ...

FEMALE CHORUS: And brushes clumps of earth from the soles of her shoes.

CASSANDRA: Oh, dear …

MALE CHORUS: He finds scraps of paper, covered in Cassandra's frenzied hand, tucked under the mattress or fluttering on the lawn: cryptic treatises overlaid with spirographic diagrams, interconnected boxes and innumerable arrows that chase each other to infinity. And at the top of each page, in tiny, adamant capitals, the heading:

BEN: Affirmations.

FEMALE CHORUS: Ben hires a private nurse and, delicately, he places baby monitors in every room of the house.

CASSANDRA: (*whispering conspiratorially*) Just in case.

MALE CHORUS: And then, one very odd night, Ben receives yet another emergency call from home.

BEN: Are you all right?

CASSANDRA: No. Really.

MALE CHORUS: Ben hurtles home to find Cassandra sitting out on the pine vérité deck, in the faux Adirondack chair, with a silver pen set and reams of white paper.

FEMALE CHORUS (AS FEMALE NURSE): (*with the baby*) Their tiny baby is sleeping in her bassinet.

MALE CHORUS: A slow wind blows at the sheets on their bed.

BEN: At Cassandra's hair.

FEMALE CHORUS: Sheets of paper dense with Cassandra's hand flutter in from the deck and tumble lazily around the room.

MALE CHORUS: The pens are drained of ink.

BEN: Sweetie?

MALE CHORUS: Cassandra gazes out over the neighbour's backyard and sees what she believes to be a deer. She has a hard time believing a deer would venture so far into the city. She blinks. She's right. It's not a deer. It is a camel. The camel tosses its head and salty froth sparkles off in all directions. The camel races into and through the neighbours' dogwood trees.

BEN: Sweetie?

FEMALE CHORUS: Ben joins Cassandra.

He strokes her hair.

BEN: Cassandra? What are you doing?

CASSANDRA: (*smiling*) I'm writing affirmations.

BEN: Affirmations?

CASSANDRA: Yes. Affirmations. They are sentences one constructs that affirm the polar opposite of an actuality, or of actualities. They are designed to trick the mind out of its reason. To bypass the soul's deepest instincts. They're a sort of mental conjuring, a kind of psychic sleight of hand.

BEN: A sort of magic.

CASSANDRA: Yes. If they work.

BEN: (*gently*) Do they work?

FEMALE CHORUS: Cassandra's mind works furiously, considering poles and their opposites. Cassandra looks into, and through, her handsome husband's shining eyes.

CASSANDRA: (*echoing, beaming*) Nothing is too wonderful to be true.

MALE CHORUS: Far across the planet, the last eucalyptus tree crashes to the ground. Though there is no forest, there are people there, and so the fall is heard.

FEMALE CHORUS: What is not heard is the sound of the tiny cryptococcus virus, whose home has been destroyed, whose tiny baby has been slaughtered, whose own huge copper eyes spill over with tears, and who now flies into the open mouth of the man with the axe and stows away, hell-bent on lashing back. It is not a monster. It is only being viral.

Pause.

BEN: What do you want?

CASSANDRA: (*giggling*) Oh, Ben, I don't know.

BEN: What do you need?

CASSANDRA: (*not giggling*) Nothing.

Little pause.

MALE CHORUS: They watch each other breathe for a moment.

CASSANDRA: (*almost seductively*) I need nothing.

FEMALE CHORUS: She touches the flesh of his cheek.

Cassandra touches Ben's cheek, then guides him towards the bassinet.

MALE CHORUS: Cassandra looks in on the baby.

FEMALE CHORUS: The baby writhes and turns away.

CASSANDRA: She opened her eyes today. And I thought that I saw them ...

BEN: ... move?

CASSANDRA: Yes. Look at her. What do you see?

BEN: I see the light of my life.

CASSANDRA: Hmmmm ...

FEMALE CHORUS: Cassandra studies the sparkles in her husband's eyes.

BEN: Penny for your thoughts?

CASSANDRA: There is a devouring blackness that has an irresistible hold on my imagination, and the pain of reflection is too much for my weak soul to bear.

BEN: I beg your pardon?

CASSANDRA: (*emphatically*) I said, 'There is a devouring blackness that has an irresistible hold on my imagination, and the pain of reflection is too much for my weak soul to bear.'

BEN: That's what I thought you said. Such a deep and cryptic girl.

CASSANDRA: Deep girls picture universes.

BEN: And now I see them too.

FEMALE CHORUS: Ben's hands tremble.

CASSANDRA: There, there.

MALE CHORUS: Cassandra kisses the backs of his hands.

She kisses the palms of his hands.

CASSANDRA: There are too many people in the world. Anyway.

She circles the room, then goes back outside.

MALE CHORUS: (*softly*) Cassandra tilts her face up to the falling sky.

Ben follows her.

FEMALE CHORUS: (*softly*) Ben watches the light play on the pulse in her throat.

Music under: a bittersweet 'Insane Song' reprise.

BEN: I brought you a gift.

CASSANDRA: Oh!

BEN: (*gently*) Open it.

MALE CHORUS: She does. It is the third in the angel doll set. It is a bit wonkier than the others, its head already backward on its body, its wings long and bedraggled, more bone than feather.

BEN: It didn't turn out exactly as I meant it but …

MALE CHORUS: A segment of wing falls off and flutters to the ground.

BEN: I didn't have as much time as I would have liked.

FEMALE CHORUS: The angel's left eye rolls back in its socket, flutters for a minute, winks, then falls into the vortex of its pink plastic skull.

CASSANDRA: Why, Ben! It's exactly like art. (*little pause*) It's dreadfully beautiful.

Ben takes a deep breath.

BEN: Open its chest and see what's inside.

FEMALE CHORUS: Cassandra examines the angel doll's chest. There are two perfect nipples, raised up. She pulls them, and two tiny doors open up.

BEN: Reach inside. There's a surprise.

CASSANDRA: A surprise?

BEN: Yes.

CASSANDRA: Oh!

FEMALE CHORUS: And inside the angel's little chest, between its ribs and spine and warm wet lungs, nestled right where the angel's heart should be …

CASSANDRA: (*little gasp*) You didn't!

FEMALE CHORUS: There is a shiny ball.

CASSANDRA: You did!

BEN: It had you written all over it.

Cassandra pulls the shiny ball from the angel's chest and dangles it. She looks into Ben's eyes.

CASSANDRA: (*softly*) Thank you, Ben. For the time you bought me.

BEN: The pleasure was all mine.

CASSANDRA: No. It wasn't. It was my pleasure too.

Pause.

BEN: Happy, darling?

CASSANDRA: (*almost a whisper*) Out of my mind.

Mathematics

FEMALE CHORUS: Later that evening. The tiny glowing baby sleeps peacefully in her bassinet.

The Female Chorus moves into nurse position. She sits protectively, with one arm draped over the bassinet.

MALE CHORUS: Cassandra looks in on the baby.

Cassandra peers into the bassinet.

MALE CHORUS: The baby cries.

FEMALE CHORUS: Cassandra moves a fuzzy cross-eyed lavender bunny a little further away from the baby.

CASSANDRA: (*parenting tip, to the audience*) So it doesn't crush her.

FEMALE CHORUS: Shhhhh.

Cassandra looks at the Female Chorus. The Female Chorus sees Cassandra, but attends to the baby. Cassandra raises her hands like a criminal and backs away.

MALE CHORUS: Then Cassandra wanders out into the emerald backyard.

She crosses the stage.

MALE CHORUS: She gazes up into the chartreuse August sky.

She looks up. She extends one hand.

CHORUS: Snow falls.

Music transition: 'Insane Song' reprise turns into 'Fly Away' instrumental. The tune is the same as 'Quicksilver' and 'Semi-Residentia,' only much softer, slower, darker.

FEMALE CHORUS: Downtown, in a granite bunker, far below the city streets, Ben addresses the CEOs of Quicksilver Unlimited.

BEN: Good evening, gentle ladies and men.

MALE CHORUS: Ben flicks a switch. On a giant screen above him, an image of a cross-eyed cow appears. The cow is a cream pitcher. Across the image of the cow, there is a big black X.

Ben looks at the audience.

BEN: Once upon a time, cows were a comfort, signifying health and well-being. Cows had the power to transport. To offer a moment's relief from an ever-present dread. But now, a cow is useless. For dread has given way to this …

MALE CHORUS: Ben gestures out –

Ben extends his arms.

FEMALE CHORUS: – indicating the world.

BEN: And now, a cow is irrelevant.

Cassandra extends her arms.

MALE CHORUS: Cassandra reaches out. To catch the falling snow.

There is a moment of stillness, as both hold their arms outstretched, Ben looking down, Cassandra gazing up.

BEN: For now we must let go of cows. The future now lies with angels.

CHORUS: (*singing, sotto voce*)

Hemlock's for the heavy heart,
The arsenic speeds it through the veins.

BEN: And angels alone.

CHORUS:

Mercury's for certainty,
The morphine's for the pain.

BEN: We have plumbed the virtues of the dirt and the trees and the seven seas – (*He shakes his head.*) I beg your pardon. The sick seas. The *six seas*.

Little pause. Ben collects himself.

BEN: We have channelled our energies into the earth. And now the earth is offering itself up to us. And we are harnessing the power of the planet to release our friends, humans who, by virtue of their humanity, have grown shackled with cares that are simply too much for their weak souls to bear.

CHORUS: (*sotto voce*)

Strychnine for the stricken quiets
Echoes of a loved one's cries …

BEN: And so, we are harvesting. Precious gifts. Gifts for those who can't get enough, and now, at last, for those who've had too much.

CHORUS: (*sotto voce*)

Cyanide will stop the days and
Weeks and months of wondering 'Why?'

BEN: I believe that in the spaces between the products there lies a truth about humanity. About what they want. What they need.

MALE CHORUS: Cassandra brings her hands toward her face and gazes at the snowflakes she has caught.

BEN: I believe it is our burden and our privilege to conjure for them.

The promise of peace. The promise of release. Through images of hope. Images of hope more powerful than hope itself.

CHORUS: (*singing*)

We live our lives unbound.

BEN: Some might accuse me of a lack of elegance – a lack of grace – speaking of such things at a time like this.

Cassandra turns to Ben. They lock eyes.

BEN: Well, this is a graceless time.

Cassandra smiles at Ben.

BEN: And there are a lot of very hopeless people out there.

CHORUS: (*singing*)
But when we tumble to the ground,

BEN: It's all mathematics. It all adds up.

CHORUS:
The extracts of the sacred earth
Themselves do offer up for our rebirth.

BEN: Simple as two and two.

CHORUS:
The mingled juices laced
With kindness, pity, mercy, love and grace.

MALE CHORUS: Cassandra tastes the snowflakes she has caught.

She brings her hand to her mouth. Ben returns his attention back to the CEO*s. Cassandra watches.*

BEN: I have ...

Ben takes a deep breath.

I have a gift box here.

FEMALE CHORUS: Ben presents a beautiful angel gift box, its flesh a phosphorous yellow, its eyes a deep shimmering black, its heart a tiny red light bulb that blinks on and off. And on a little oyster-grey cushion where the angel's liver should be, there is a glimmering shiny ball.

MALE CHORUS: The CEOs coo with delight.

ALL:

Hemlock's for the heavy heart,
The arsenic speeds it through the veins.
Mercury's for certainty,
The morphine's for the pain.
These mingled juices laced
With kindness, pity, mercy, love and grace.

BEN:

Kindness, pity,
Mercy, love and …

CASSANDRA: *(right to Ben)*
Kindness, sweetness,
Mercy, love and …

ALL:

Kindness, sweetness, mercy, love and grace.

Music out. The rest of the play is performed with very little movement. The feeling is of a lifting of something; that is, the mood becomes genuinely light. Gem-coloured lights flood the stage.

Sleep-swimming

FEMALE CHORUS: Cassandra hangs her shiny ball around her pale neck. She drifts across her emerald lawn, down her faux flagstone driveway, past a huddle of sleeping retrievers –

CASSANDRA: Shhhhh.

FEMALE CHORUS: – and slips, undetected, out into the street.

MALE CHORUS: She winds her way expertly through the snowy labyrinth of Semi-Residentia, shivering happily in her thin nightgown.

FEMALE CHORUS: She walks and walks until the office towers loom into view and the narrow streets return her to the sparkling boulevards.

MALE CHORUS: She steals past the smoky clubs and peers in at thrushes of dreamy, drifting bodies, dancing close.

FEMALE CHORUS: She strolls past a hospital where nurses in white dresses wander down the endless lineup to emergency and murmur into fevered ears about the passage to the light.

MALE CHORUS: She drifts through herds of teenage girls feeling fancy in white slip dresses, their brand new shiny balls dangling from their slender teenage necks.

FEMALE CHORUS (AS TEENAGE GIRL): Just in case …

FEMALE CHORUS: Cassandra tiptoes by the cash-strapped newlywed couple, who sit naked on a boardwalk bench, dangling their icy toes and tracing budgets in the sand.

MALE CHORUS: The newlyweds exchange pearl-grey gift boxes from which each pulls a shiny ball that dangles and spins from its delicate chain.

FEMALE CHORUS (AS NEWLYWED WOMAN): (*gleefully*) You didn't!

MALE CHORUS (AS NEWLYWED MAN): (*gratefully*) You did!

FEMALE CHORUS: Cassandra walks into a bus shelter where there is a glowing, larger-than-life photo of a hollow-cheeked, hollow-eyed man.

The Male Chorus embodies the man.

FEMALE CHORUS: A shiny ball hangs from around his neck.

Cassandra moves toward him.

FEMALE CHORUS: The inscription beneath the photo reads:

CASSANDRA: Bury: Artist.

FEMALE CHORUS: In Abyss khakis and pocket T.

MALE CHORUS: Cassandra goes to the photograph and touches the image. She kisses it on the lips.

Cassandra and the Male Chorus embrace.

FEMALE CHORUS: Then Cassandra steps back and sees her red lipstick imprint on a full-colour photo of brilliant white facial tissues.

MALE CHORUS: (*in voice-over voice*) Soft as nothing.

Music in: 'Snow Song' reprise. The Male Chorus turns Cassandra toward the graveyard.

CHORUS: Snow falls.

Cassandra watches the Male Chorus walk toward the Female Chorus. From now on, the stage directions are instructive for Cassandra, as the Chorus guides her toward the end.

FEMALE CHORUS: Cassandra walks and walks.

MALE CHORUS: She walks and walks.

FEMALE CHORUS: She walks until she reaches the graveyard gates.

MALE CHORUS: Then Cassandra closes her thick-lashed eyes …

FEMALE CHORUS: – and deep in the dove-grey coils of her brain, neurons and dendrites shimmer and spiral and speed around her fathomless mind.

MALE CHORUS: A hundred blocks away, Ben ascends from the granite bunker to hail a taxi.

FEMALE CHORUS: Ben gets into the taxi, stepping lightly over a good intention that has ruckled up in the road.

MALE CHORUS (AS TAXI DRIVER): Nice night.

Lights shift and become more icy.

MALE CHORUS: The graveyard is flooded, as a recent soar in temperature is now melting the August snowflakes even as they fall.

FEMALE CHORUS: Grieving citizens, adorned with new and gleaming shiny balls, drift through the graveyard gates.

MALE CHORUS: They descend a gentle slope until the water swirls around their hips, and then they dive in, searching for their loved ones' graves.

FEMALE CHORUS: The water level rises as tears mingle with the melting snow.

MALE CHORUS: Cassandra descends into the graveyard until the water swirls around her waist. She dives in. She paddles through a sea of mourners and embraces a gravestone as though it were alive. Her shiny ball bobs in the water and tickles at her cheek.

FEMALE CHORUS: Cassandra unscrews the tiny pin that anchors the shiny ball to its delicate chain. And she stares into the void.

CASSANDRA: Bless you, pet. A drop for me.

FEMALE CHORUS: Then, from out of the blackness, or out of the blue –

MALE CHORUS: – from the chasmic shadows of the glimmering megalopolis –

BEN: – office workers, manicurists and accountants stream into the graveyard wearing cappuccino chinos and ribbed halter tops.

CASSANDRA: Telemarketers, waiters and switchboard operators dive into the water in white pocket Ts and black turtlenecks.

FEMALE CHORUS: Each one sports a brand-new shiny ball that shimmers and gleams in the slate-grey night.

MALE CHORUS: Each one swims to a gravestone.

BEN: Each one tries to unwind dread from love.

CASSANDRA: Each one sings love words to someone who is gone.

ALL: It is an orgy of unrequited love.

The performers sing the 'Insane Song' reprise, and execute, en place, *a fifties-girl-group-style dance sequence featuring snippets of aquatically inspired dances such as the Swim, the Sink and the Dive. The dance is joyous, a celebration. The lights, like the dance moves, are beautiful. Music soars.*

ALL:

I will give the hand I gave before
And give the one I kept myself,
To keep a grip and save my soul
From plunging in the wishing well.
For though my thoughts run round the world,
And faster than this spinning plane,
When reason reaches out for me,
It's you who calls me back again.
And though I swore I'd never slip
Back in the cosmic dizzy spell,
I'm slipping, falling for you, dear,
With all my heart, my love's unquelled.

ALL:

Though it may seem a bit insane,
I can't help but feel a love for
Which I cannot find a name.

Dance break.

MALE CHORUS: Then, just as the warmth begins to flood her veins, and the tangles to slip from her fathomless mind, Ben dives into the water and swims to Cassandra's side.

Cassandra and Ben come together and stay that way for the rest of the show.

FEMALE CHORUS: He gently unwraps her arms from the gravestone and swims her, half-poisoned, half-drowned, to the high roof of a mausoleum.

MALE CHORUS: Her opened, emptied shiny ball bobs on the water's surface.

FEMALE CHORUS: It floats away.

ALL:

Though it may seem a bit insane …

Music out.

Pluto and the Moons of Mars

FEMALE CHORUS: On the roof of the tomb.

sfx: marvellous crickets.

CASSANDRA: What's your favourite planet?

Ben does not speak.

CASSANDRA: Tell me, Ben. I want to know.

BEN: Pluto.

CASSANDRA: Why?

BEN: Because of its name.

CASSANDRA: Why?

BEN: Because its name reminds me of dogs and bright colours. Its name makes me feel as though the planet itself has a personality. Like a dog. It diverts my mind from the fact that the planet is too cold for human inhabitance and reminds me of dogs and bright colours. What's yours?

CASSANDRA: Mars.

BEN: Because it's warm and glowing?

CASSANDRA: Because it has two moons: Deimos and Phobos.

BEN: Meaning?

CASSANDRA: Meaning dread and fear.

BEN: Oh.

CASSANDRA: Two moons like that could keep a girl like me company. Make a girl like me feel a little less alone.

BEN: Don't I make you feel less alone?

CASSANDRA: Depends on my mood.

BEN: Are your eyes seeing both ways again, my pet?

CASSANDRA: Oh, yes.

BEN: Then close them. What do you see?

CASSANDRA: What do you think?

BEN: Then wrap your arms around me. What do you feel?

CASSANDRA: I feel warm flesh filled with living motion.

BEN: Kiss my lips. What do you taste?

CASSANDRA: The elixir of life. Bite my tongue.

BEN: Salt springs from it.

CASSANDRA: Like from the six seas. Smell my hair.

BEN: I smell the jungle. I smell papaya.

CASSANDRA: Sniff my neck.

BEN: I smell pine cones and musk.

CASSANDRA: Sniff this whisper.

BEN: I smell fear.

CASSANDRA: Yes …

BEN: And dread …

CASSANDRA: Yes …

BEN: And … lipstick. You are a heady cocktail, my love.

CASSANDRA: But will I always be?

BEN: Oh, yes.

CASSANDRA: Oh … no …

Cassandra and Ben hold in an embrace. Their lips are very close.

MALE CHORUS: Ben holds Cassandra's hand, strokes her forehead and sings to her about the marvellous universe that is her tangled mind, the astonishing power of the transformative lenses through which he now sees the world, the horrible radiance of her shuddering body, the marvels of the strange perfection of the physiological systems within them, the magic of the life that courses through his veins and slips now from hers.

FEMALE CHORUS: Ben kisses Cassandra's mind.

MALE CHORUS: She heaves her final huge exhalation.

FEMALE CHORUS: And Cassandra flies away.

MALE CHORUS: She floats above the graveyard, above streets and backyards, and soars past the office towers and up into the clouds.

FEMALE CHORUS: She sails past the bank manager in his smashed-up car, still speaking love words to his pie-baking wife –

MALE CHORUS: – and past the naked, cash-strapped newlyweds, ascending the nimbi and the strata hand in hand, blissfully chasing a skittering hundred-dollar bill.

FEMALE CHORUS: Cassandra wings through the atmosphere and beholds flurries of angels –

MALE CHORUS: – who look exactly like Ben's angel dolls – in every curious detail.

The Chorus moves to the centre of the stage, in the style of Teatro en Atril, *as at the play's start. Ben and Cassandra very delicately untangle themselves from each other and join the Chorus at centre stage.*

FEMALE CHORUS: Cassandra watches as the world spins faster and faster and turns from green and blue to taupe with humanity.

MALE CHORUS: She watches as Surely grows into a tiny, perfect toddler, swaddled by her daddy in cunning ensembles: Baby Abyss.

MALE CHORUS: She watches as Quicksilver Unlimited grows into a chain that wraps right around the world and takes steady steps toward soothing the planet painless.

FEMALE CHORUS: Cassandra watches till the delicate physical properties that order the fragile chemistry of creation fold their cards, slide them under the earth's four corners, then peel away the edges.

MALE CHORUS: Till the air grows thick with wild-eyed zebras, wonderstruck people and exquisite purple copper-eyed cryptococci –

FEMALE CHORUS: – with fuzzy camels, cross-eyed octopi and majestic golden retrievers, as they, and all the wilderness and seas, fly off the earth.

MALE CHORUS: Sacred offerings from the centre of the universe.

FEMALE CHORUS: Until the spinning blue globe in the midst of red Mars, lime-green Saturn and golden Pluto is rendered, at last, a shimmering, whirling, silvery shiny ball.

BEN: And the angels sing:

Singing, as angel dolls, in three-part harmony.

BEN AND CHORUS:

Heaven, I'm in heaven,
And my heart beats so that I can hardly spe-e-e-eak.

Pause.

ALL: (in *four-part harmony*)

Though it may seem a bit insane,
I'll forever feel a love

For which I cannot
Find
A …

They gasp. They look up and out.

ALL: (*softly*) Look at the sky!

Snow Song

Cassandra
Piano
Lightly
mp
Seems the sky has fal- len down,
Stars have tumb- led to the ground.
I'd make a wish 'cept I'm bid- ding wish- ing too- dle- oo.
I've on ly got one wish, and it's nev- er com- ing tru ...
... ue.
I'd wish the world's dark- est mys- ter- y would come up clear:
Why it's the spar- kl- ing

Cassandra
Piano
things that al- ways dis- ap- pear. But
that'd be like wish- ing that two and two made five. That'd be like wish- ing that
you, my dear, were still a- live. My swee- tie pie.
On- ly you will ev- er be my hon- ey lamb.
On- ly you, but there you are and here I am.

continues ...

The Shiny Ball Song

Cassandra
In the midst of a- ny mess there is a shi- ny ball.
Ben
Kit- tens! In the midst of a- ny mess there is a shi- ny ball.
Piano

Cassandra
I'm so glad that you're the same as I'm so glad that you're the same as me-e-e- eee.
Ben
I'm so glad that you're the same as I'm so glad that you're the same as me-e-e- eee.
Piano

More Snow

F Chorus
M Chorus
Piano
Gently ♩=78
mp
Ah ah, Oh ah ah, Oh Ah ah, Oh ah ah, Oh,
Cassandra
Ben
Seems the sky is fall- ing down, Stars are tumb- ing all a- round.
Ah ah, Oh ah ah, Oh ah ah, Oh ah ah, Oh ah ah, Oh ah ah, Oh ah ah, Oh ah ah, Oh!
Ah!
I'll make a wish, and a lit- tle psy- chic switch- e- roo.
And when all the stars have fal- len through the

Cassandra
Ben
F Chorus
M Chorus
Piano
black- ness of the sky, And hissed their fin- al sigh-
Seems my wish can't help but come true.
Ah- aahh,
Can't help but come true.
3

The Abyss

Cassandra
Piano
Just give your flesh to me and I'll a- dorn it ex- pert- ly, And doom and dread will fall in tat- ters to the
floor. Though the styles might seem out- ra- geous, trust my pro- mise is sa- ga- cious: You'll feel bet- ter than you did before.
F Chorus
M Chorus
When she stares in- to my eyes, I'm tran- quil- ized. My knees get mel- ty and my eyes they
8ve....
blur ... 'Cuz I'm soar- ing o'er a chas- m that looks some- thing like nir- van- a – I'd go
a- ny- where with her.

Cassandra
F Chorus
M Chorus
Piano
Love- ly things can make this bleak life worth the griev- ing. In-
Jing- ly rings!
spire the will to keep on breath-ing. When your dreams lie dashed in shreds like last year's dress, catch the gifts that
Ah Oh Ah Oh Ah Oh Ah Oh Ah Oh Ah Oh
Lightly
fall to you from noth- ing- ness.
Ah Oh Ah Oh
Sweat- ers soft as snow come spil- ling from the shelves,
Slowly ♩=60
Dream- i- er than dreams them- sel- ves ...
Tempo ♩=110

continues ...

Consummation

F Chorus
M Chorus
Piano
Touch me, baby, touch me slowly, touch me, honey, Make me sigh. Touch me quick, before it's too late, touch me now so I don't cry.
Look how strong his gentle hands are, look at that forearm of his, which, when it's pressed against your flesh, looks bigger than it really is.

continues ...

Quicksilver

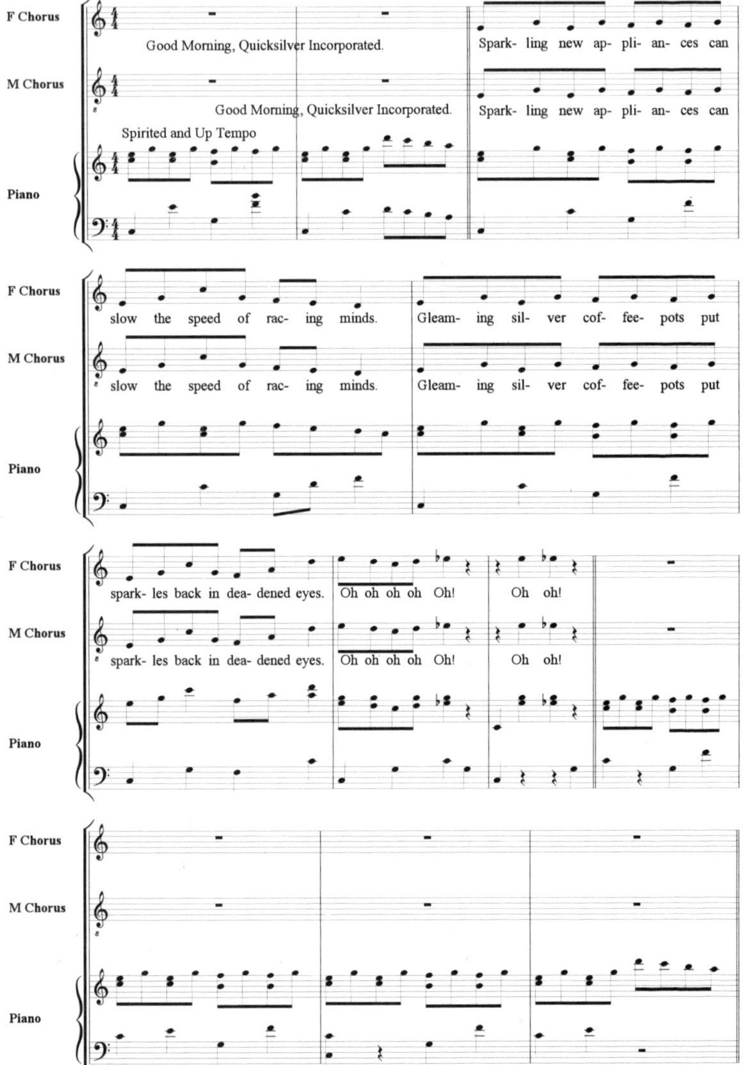

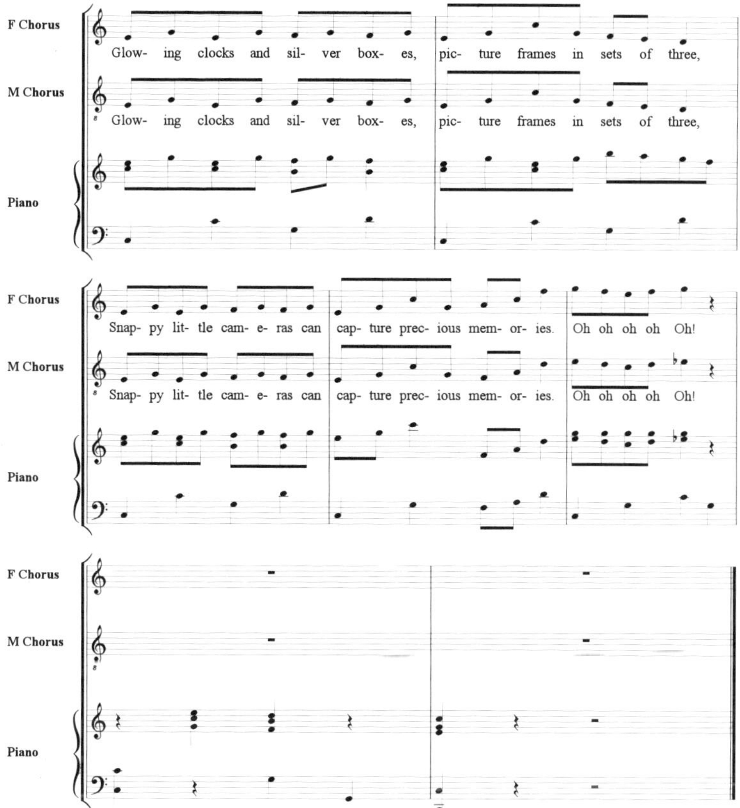
F Chorus
M Chorus
Piano
Glow- ing clocks and sil- ver box- es, pic- ture frames in sets of three,
Glow- ing clocks and sil- ver box- es, pic- ture frames in sets of three,
F Chorus
M Chorus
Piano
Snap- py lit- tle cam- e- ras can cap- ture prec- ious mem- or- ies. Oh oh oh oh Oh!
Snap- py lit- tle cam- e- ras can cap- ture prec- ious mem- or- ies. Oh oh oh oh Oh!
F Chorus
M Chorus
Piano

Insane Song

Ben
Piano
Pop Ballad
With lots of love
Let me smooth your trou- bled brow and
pull the tan- gles from your mind, and
though I'm some- what ter- ri- fied of
all the knots I know I'll find, I'm
sure on earth we live but once, be-
fore the night comes sweep- ing by. So
give your hand, my sweet, or else I
may not wake be- fore I die.
Though it may seem a- a bit in- sane,
I can't help but feel a love for which I can- not find a name.
Cassandra
I will give the hand I gave be- fore and give the one I kept my- self, to keep a grip and save my

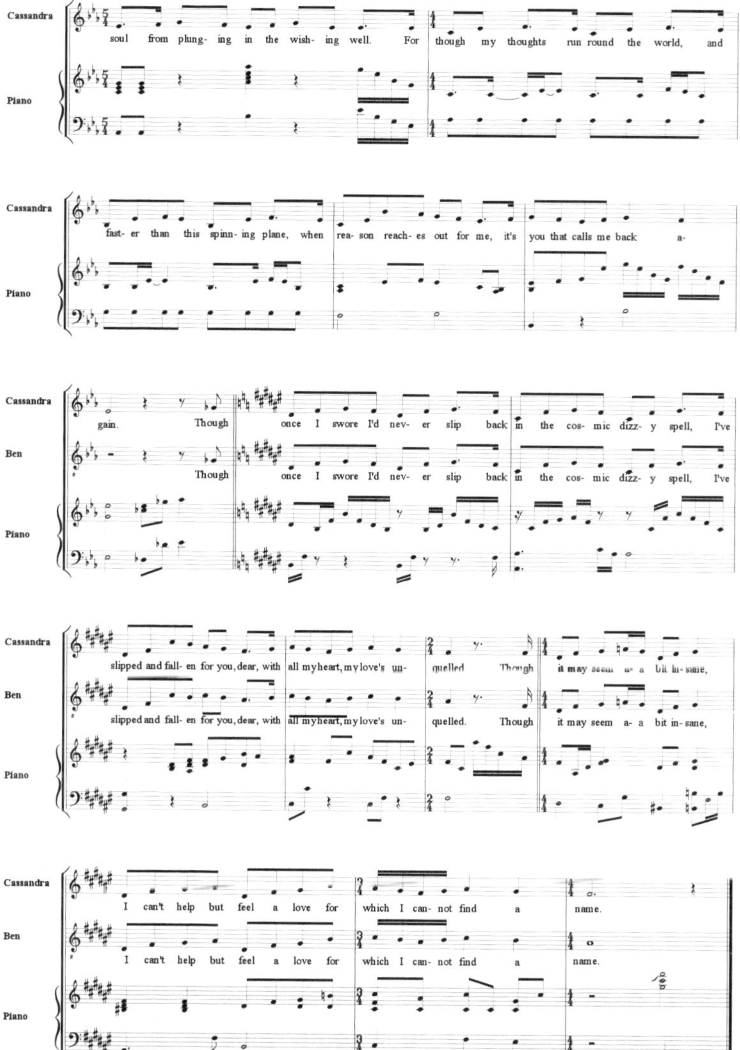
Cassandra
Piano
soul from plung- ing in the wish- ing well. For though my thoughts run round the world, and
fast- er than this spinn- ing plane, when rea- son reach- es out for me, it's you that calls me back a-
gain. Though once I swore I'd nev- er slip back in the cos- mic dizz- y spell, I've
Ben
Though once I swore I'd nev- er slip back in the cos- mic dizz- y spell, I've
slipped and fall- en for you, dear, with all my heart, my love's un- quelled. Though it may seem a- a bit in- sane,
slipped and fall- en for you, dear, with all my heart, my love's un- quelled. Though it may seem a- a bit in- sane,
I can't help but feel a love for which I can- not find a name.
I can't help but feel a love for which I can- not find a name.

When a Rabbit Dies

Cassandra
F Chorus
M Chorus
Piano
When a bun- ny dies, a girl can't help but feel a
Doom doom doom!
Doom doom doom doo-bee-doo-bee
lit- tle sad for the con- vul- sing rab- bit.
But a
Ben
For a bun- ny's terr- or as its life slips a- way,
But a
rab- bit's ru- in marks our bright- est day!
(Faster and Brighter)

continues ...

In Semi-Residentia

Cry, Cry, Cry

F Chorus
M Chorus
Piano
Driving and Urgent
mf
Feel the wild thing in the black- ness,
feel it wrig- gle, feel it writhe.
Feel its neck, which, when it moves, grows tangl- ed in the ties that bind.
Feel it thrash its pur- ple legs and pur- ple arms, they're built to swim.

F Chorus
Feel it wrest- le, feel it pan- ic, Bab- y needs some ox-
M Chorus
Feel it wrest- le, feel it pan- ic, Bab- y needs some ox-
Piano
Ben
F Chorus
y- gen! Come on, bab- y, come on, hone- y,
M Chorus
y- gen! Come on, bab- y, come on, hone- y,
Ben
Come on, bab- y, come on, hone- y,
Piano
Ben
Come on down in- to the light. Smell how sweet and strange the air is,
F Chorus
Come on down in- to the light. Smell how sweet and strange the air is,
M Chorus
Come on down in- to the light. Smell how sweet and strange the air is,
Piano
Ben
take a breath and cry cry cry!
F Chorus
take a breath and cry cry cry!
M Chorus
take a breath and cry cry cry!
Piano

Smaller and Stranger

F Chorus
M Chorus
Piano
an- gel hairs.
An- gel hairs.
Out of the dark-ness she's flung.
How does the air find her lungs?
Must be some-thing in the breeze that makes this crea- ture
yearn to breathe.
Cassandra
Smal- ler and strang- er is she,
smal- ler and strang- er than we.
But
look at how her lit- tle hands make fists I some- how un- der-stand.

continues ...

Fly Away

continues ...

Acknowledgements

Hello … Hello, like many musical plays, experienced several incarnations. Ultimately, it is the spawn of a fifteen-minute 'office play' called *Telemarketing: the Musical* that was created for Tarragon's Spring Arts Fair while I was a member of the Tarragon Playwrights' Unit in 1994. From 1994 to 1996, Greg Morrison and I developed the piece as a full scale twelve-person musical called *La BOOM*, with the Tarragon's support. *La BOOM* also received support, through public and private workshops, from Canadian Stage, the Women in View Festival and the Banff playRites Colony.

In 1996, with gratitude to all who had championed it, I abandoned *La BOOM* with the recognition that what I had been writing was a lavish production whose content would probably never warrant a lavish musical budget. I embarked on a radical revision of the text for an ensemble of four who would play a cast of thousands: *Hello … Hello*.

Hello … Hello was supported at all stages of its development by the Toronto Arts Council, the Ontario Arts Council, the Canada Council for the Arts and the Laidlaw Foundation. Financial support also came, at times, from my parents, Bernice and Colin Hines, and from James Edmond.

For this work, I have travelled with many collaborators, some for short distances, some for the whole path. It is difficult to express enough appreciation for their inspired work, their support, inspiration and patience.

The following participated as performers in *La BOOM*: Jennifer Dean, Paulina Gillis, Wendy Hopkins, Douglas McNaughton, Christine Oddy, Paul O'Sullivan, Jennifer Parsons, Ed Roy, Ed Sahely, Jonathan Wilson. Andy McKim and Peter Hinton directed the *La BOOM* workshops. Erica Heyland was stage manager. Urjo Kareda, Iris Turcott, Candice Berley and Joann McIntyre participated dramaturgically in the developmental workshops of *La BOOM*.

Greg Morrison was musical director and composer for every stage of development. Chris Earle was the director and dramaturge for each phase once it became *Hello … Hello*. Steve Morel performed in each and every version, including *Telemarketing: the Musical*, in which he co-starred with his wife, Jennifer Parsons. They, along with the performers and crew at all stages of development, proved that 'nothing is too wonderful to be true.'

The *Hello … Hello* stage managers were Melissa Berney, Alison Peddy and Sarah Baumann. Through various stages of *Hello … Hello*'s development and production, Heather Morton, Ken Gass, Layne Coleman, Brian Quirt, David Smukler, Vikki Anderson, Nancy Webster, Naomi Campbell, John Thompson and Michel Charbonneau contributed as designers, producers and valued consultants.

For inspiration and support, I owe debts to the Hines family, Gordon Tisdall, Ted Hughes, Sylvia Plath, Marshall McLuhan, Puccini, Kalle Lasn, Mary Shelley, Richard Rose, Mallory Gilbert, Sandra Balcovske, Eileen Smith, Richard Pochinko, Ian Wallace, Michael Kennard, John Turner, Susan Zucker, Kathleen Oliver, Blake Brooker, James Edmond and Shirley Faessler.

Thanks to Kiran Sachdev for his fine work on the music in this book, and to Peter Moller for his horribly beautiful cover design.

I am grateful to my editor at Coach House Books, Christina Palassio, for her painstaking care. Also to senior editor Alana Wilcox for choosing to make this play into a book. Blessings to all the people at Coach House Books who make the books.

Rabbit Footnote

In the late 1920s, it was discovered that when a female rabbit was injected with a pregnant woman's urine (which contains an elevated level of human chorionic gonadotropin), the injection would result in *corpora hemorrhagica* in the ovaries of the rabbit. These bulging masses on the bunny's ovaries could not be seen without killing and dissecting the rabbit to inspect the ovaries, so, in fact, every rabbit died during a pregnancy test, even if the woman wasn't pregnant. Curiously, and regardless of the scientific facts, a rabbit's death came to be linked, symbolically and euphemistically, to the impending birth of a human child.

Biographies

KAREN HINES is an award-winning writer, director and performer and the artistic director and producer of Keep Frozen: Pochsy Productions. Her acclaimed Pochsy monologues, *Pochsy's Lips*; *Oh, baby;* and *Citizen Pochsy,* have been performed at venues across North America. Collected by Coach House Books in 2004 as *The Pochsy Plays*, these monologues earned Karen a Gwen Pharis Ringwood Alberta Writer's Guild Award and a nomination for the 2004 Governor General's Award for Drama. Karen is also the long-time director of horror clowns Mump & Smoot and a Gemini-nominated actor who has starred in several of Ken Finkleman's television satires, including *The Newsroom*. For more information, please go to www.pochsy.org.

GREG MORRISON began working in theatre as the musical director for the Second City Touring Company. His composing and musical director credits include *Pochsy's Lips*; *Oh, baby*; *Citizen Pochsy* and *Pochsy Unplugged*, as well as the Mump & Smoot shows *Something Else* and *Flux*. Greg was also the composer and book writer for *The Age of Dorian* and the composer, with Lisa Lambert, for *The Drowsy Chaperone*, from the Canadian Fringe to Broadway. He has composed extensively for television and radio, including music for *Getting Along Famously* (CBC) and *Slings and Arrows* (Rhombus).

Typeset in Granjon and printed and bound at the Coach House on bpNichol Lane, 2006.

Edited by Christina Palassio
Cover design by Peter Moller
Musical scores by Greg Morrison

Coach House Books
401 Huron St. (rear) on bpNichol Lane
Toronto, Ontario
M5S 2G5

416 979 2217
1 800 367 6360

mail@chbooks.com
www.chbooks.com